Picture Perfect

Framing

Picture Perfect
Framing

Making
Matting
Mounting
Embellishing
Displaying
& More

Katie DuMont

LARK BOOKS
A Division of Sterling Publishing Co., Inc.
New York

Art Director: Tom Metcalf
Production: Tom Metcalf, Kathy Holmes
Production Assistant: Hannes Charen, Heather Smith
Photography: Projects, Evan Bracken, How-tos, Richard Hasselberg
Photo Stylist and Props: Dana Irwin
Illustrations: Olivier Rollins
Photography and illustrations in frames on pages 54, 56, 71, 72, 75, 78, 82, 86, 88, 94, and front cover by Dana Irwin

Library of Congress Cataloging-in-Publication Data

DuMont, Katie.
   Picture perfect framing: making, matting, mounting,
embellishing, displaying, & more / Katie DuMont.
     p. cm.
   Includes index.
   ISBN 1-57990-165-4 (hardcover) 1-57990-311-8 (paperback)
    1. Picture frames and framing. I. Title

N8550 .D86 2000
749'.7—dc21

                00-028227
                   CIP
10 9 8 7 6 5 4 3 2 1

Published by Lark Books, a division of
Sterling Publishing Co., Inc.
387 Park Avenue South, New York, N.Y. 10016

© 2000, Lark Books

Distributed in Canada by Sterling Publishing,
c/o Canadian Manda Group, One Atlantic Ave., Suite 105
Toronto, Ontario, Canada M6K 3E7

Distributed in the U.K. by:
Guild of Master Craftsman Publications Ltd.
Castle Place, 166 High Street, Lewes East Sussex, England BN7 1XU
Tel: (+ 44) 1273 477374, Fax: (+ 44) 1273 478606,
Email: pubs@thegmcgroup.com, Web: www.gmcpublications.com

Distributed in Australia by Capricorn Link (Australia) Pty Ltd., P.O. Box 704, Windsor, NSW
2756 Australia

If you have questions or comments about this book, please contact:
Lark Books
67 Broadway
Asheville, NC 28801
(828) 236-9730

Printed in China

ISBN 1-57990-165-4 (hardcover) 1-57990-311-8 (paperback)

CONTENTS

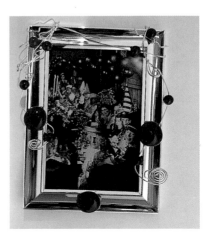

Introduction

Whether it is art that moves us more than words or last year's vacation photos, the pictures on our walls make our worlds brighter and remind us who we are. It's time we regarded what we frame with a bit more care; after all our framed art and pictures will very likely outlive our couches, dining room tables, and bedside lamps. So, if you want to do more than just fill up your wall space, there is a wealth of creative expression to be enjoyed in the art and craft of picture framing.

For your convenience this book is divided into three sections. In the first section, Anatomy of a Frame-Up, we'll examine each of the elements of the frame package—frame, glazing, mat, mount board, backing board, paper dust cover, bumpers, wire and hanging hardware, as well as hinges, tapes, and adhesives. Next, we'll learn how to make a frame from store-bought moulding, and how to put together thumbnails and sectionals too. We'll learn how to cut glass, how to select and cut a mat, and a variety of ways to mount artwork. We'll learn how to put together the entire frame package, and we'll examine the standard sizes of materials and see how the sizes relate to each other. All the necessary tools and materials are discussed in detail, and there's plenty of advice and tricks-of-the-trade shared along the way.

The second section, Picture Perfect Projects, offers 22 fun and fashionable projects for embellishing and decorating frames. From mosaics to leather to nuts and bolts to lace...there's something for everyone. Browse a bit and get inspired. The projects not only give you ideas for finishing store-bought and junk shop frames, but also show you nifty new ways to display your frames.

The third section, Hanging It Up, offers tried-and-true techniques for home decorating with framed art and pictures. If you've ever felt intimidated by a blank wall, go directly to page 90. You'll be decorating your space like a professional in no time.

Throughout the course of this book you will see terms such as, conservation, museum quality, acid-free, and archival. These terms refer to the special procedures and materials that are now being used to minimize the deteriorating effects of the natural and material environments on paper art. Conservation framing techniques and materials are more costly, but should be used whenever there is a high priority on preservation and protection. Original artwork, limited editions, works of high monetary value, rare and historical documents, treasured keepsakes, and precious family photographs are all candidates for conservation framing. Obviously, not every framing project warrants this kind of treatment. It's important to weigh all your options when framing pictures. Always consider the value of your artwork, the cost of the framing, and making a presentation that visually pleases you. One final note—nothing lasts forever, nor is it intended to. Enjoy what you have and treat it with reasonable care.

anatomy of a frame-up

The Frame Package

Figure 1 shows the basic elements of a *frame package*. The purpose of this package is to protect and enhance the enclosed artwork. The package can and should seal out dust, moisture, UV light, and insects...and provide a safe means of handling. You may not have all of these elements in a particular frame package—for instance, you don't have to use a mat, nor is glazing always required, but you should be familiar with each. Let's not forget as we examine the frame package that the most important element is the picture or artwork that the package protects.

Frame: A frame is made from (generally four) pieces of picture frame moulding joined together to form a decorative and protective support for a picture or work of art. Frames are generally rectangular or square and made from wood or metal moulding.

Glazing: Glass or acrylic is used to protect the work of art. Glass is used most often, but there are numerous occasions where frame-quality acrylic is preferable. Glazing is available with a variety of enhancements such as non-glare, anti-reflective, and ultra-violet filtering. Valuable art should never come in direct contact with glazing.

Mat: A mat is a special cardboard with a beveled opening or window cut into it, through which the artwork is displayed. The primary purpose of the mat is to separate the artwork from direct contact with the glass. This separation provides the necessary air space to help protect the picture from moisture and mold. The secondary purpose of the mat is to enhance the beauty of the artwork by providing a decorative border.

Mount board: This is a rigid board onto which the art or picture is "mounted." The mount board prevents a photo or picture from rippling and gives it a smooth, professional look. A variety of mounting methods exist. Your choice will depend on the type of artwork, the style of matting you use, and whether convenience or conservation is your priority.

Back board: This layer provides a rigid back support for the package. Back board should add strength, but not weight, and it should resist warping. Acid-free foam core and mat board are often used, as well as acid-free corrugated cardboard. Back board is held in place with brads or glazier points.

Dust cover: This layer, also referred to as *barrier paper*, keeps out dust and insects. Generally, acid-free brown kraft paper is used and is glued or adhered to the back of the frame with double-sided tape. To tighten a freshly applied dust cover, lightly spray the paper with water and allow to air-dry.

Bumpers: Protective rubber or felt pads are attached to the bottom corners of the frame to keep it from resting flat against the wall. This space between the frame and the wall allows air circulation, which helps inhibit the growth of mold and mildew. Bumpers also help keep the frame from shifting position and protect your walls. (If you suspend your picture in some nontraditional way, you may need to put bumpers on the upper corners as well.)

Hanging hardware: Hardware is attached to the back of a frame generally in the form of two screw eyes. Wire is strung between the two screw eyes and the picture is hung from this wire on a picture hanger that has been nailed into the wall.

A variety of tapes and adhesive products are used as "ribbon" to tie the package all together. Acid-free products should be considered for all framing work.

Now that we know the basic anatomy, let's take a closer look at frames.

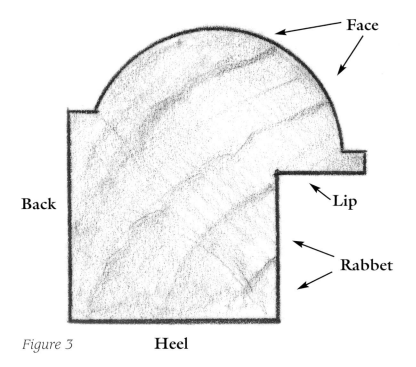

Face

Back

Lip

Rabbet

Figure 3   **Heel**

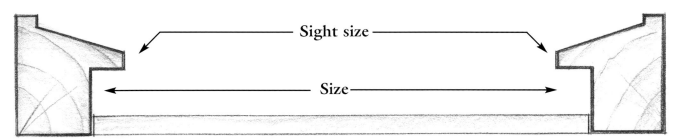

Sight size

Size

Figure 4

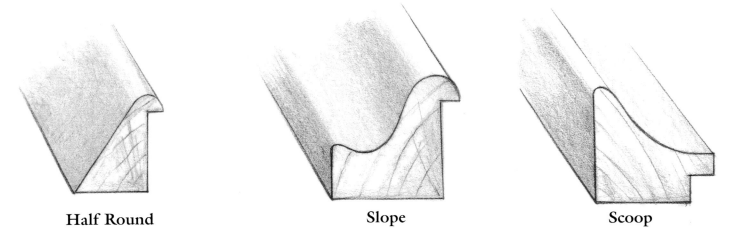

Half Round   **Slope**   **Scoop**

2. The inside edge is higher than the outside edge. The effect here is rather bold, in that the framed object appears to be pushed out from the wall. See the *Slope* profile in figure 2.

3. The outside edge is higher than the inside edge. This effect focuses attention on the picture by drawing the viewer's eye in toward the object. See the *High-Backed Bevel* profile in figure 2.

You can purchase frames in a number of ways. You can buy a ready-made, assembled frame either finished or unfinished. You can order a custom-made frame cut to your specifications. You can purchase a ready-to-assemble (a metal sectional frame sold in sets, or a custom-chopped thumbnail) frame. Finally, you can buy an uncut length of pre-finished or unfinished molding that you cut, join, and finish (if necessary) yourself.

When purchasing a ready-made frame, and your taste exceeds your budget, avoid cheap imitations of expensive ones. Choose simple, dark, wooden frames and you won't go wrong. Scour junk shops, antique markets, and estate sales for old wooden frames. You can usually refurbish sturdy old wooden frames for a fraction of the cost of new.

Choose a frame based on *what* you're going to put in it, not *where* you're going to put it.

If you choose a frame style that is distinctly suited to the art, you can hang that picture anywhere. However, if you fashion the framing to the style and decor of a particular room, you limit your decorating flexibility.

For inspiration and ideas, visit art galleries and upscale gift boutiques and note the framing choices. Start paying close attention to framed art in magazines, movies, the homes of your friends, and the businesses you frequent. Your appreciation for well-framed pictures and artwork will grow, and you'll develop your own sense of what you like and don't like.

What you are framing should influence how you frame it. For instance:

Mirrors lend themselves to heavy, bold, dominating, attention-getting frames. Highly ornate frames that tend to overpower pictures are often better suited to mirrors.

Reproductions regardless of the medium, are traditionally framed, as their originals would be. Of course, you can opt for a modern style.

Watercolors are generally framed with thinner more delicate frames, although the mats tend to be wider.

Pastels are usually framed like watercolors except little or no matting is required. (Pastels must not come in direct contact with glazing. If you opt not to mat, you must use spacers to create a cushion of air between the glass and art.)

Prints, (including lithographs, photographs, etchings, woodcuts, silk screens, and phototransfers) are commonly framed with narrow wood or metal mouldings. Black, silver, and gold are popular colors that usually don't compete with the subject matter. Matting is often white or a shade of white, and can be wide and deep.

Oil paintings generally feature more decorative frames. Be sure you select frames with deep rabbets (*Hockey Stick profiles*) that are strong and rigid enough to support the canvas. A warped canvas can lead to cracked paint. Glazing is not necessary.

Rules and Regulations

When it comes to framing, there are plenty of rules regarding "right" and "wrong". Some of these rules make perfect sense and are helpful guides. Others may seem rigid and unreasonable. All are bendable and some are made to be broken. You'll need to decide which to follow and which to ignore, based on your personal tastes, the type of artwork you have, and the environment in which you'll be hanging your picture. Let's review some of the more popular codes:

1. When framing a collection, use frames that are all the same—at least the same colors.

2. A picture in a frame that is too small loses significance.

3. Traditionally, frames do not call attention to themselves, nor do they detract attention from the picture or painting they contain. Moreover, a frame must never cramp or crowd a picture.

4. An uncomplicated painting generally calls for a plain frame.

5. A richly detailed composition is best suited for a more ornate frame.

6. Pictures with predominantly warm tones (reds, browns, and yellows) should be framed with similarly toned mouldings.

7. Pictures with predominantly cool tones (blues, greens, blue-blacks, and whites) are most likely a good match for silver or cool-toned frames.

8. A frame should complement the size, color and style of a picture. (This is generally regarded as a golden rule of framing—so think twice before breaking it.)

9. All paintings and reproductions should be framed in the style of the period they were created.

10. All oil paintings should have gilded frames.

11. All watercolors should have narrow frames and wide mats.

12. All graphic prints should have black frames and white mats.

Framing Felonies

It's true that a strong frame and an assertive mat can help a small picture look big, but this has encouraged quite an unattractive tendency to *overframe*. Just because you may have a lot of wall space to work with, doesn't mean it's a good idea to subject a prosaic print to a triple or quadruple mat job and a ridiculously ornate monster frame.

Protecting Your Art

If you want museum quality conservation standards for your framing projects, you should know that wood itself is acidic. Over time, the acid from a wooden frame can damage and discolor paper and fiber. To protect your art from the acid in a wooden frame, professional picture framers suggest applying a coat of clear acrylic sealer or polyester tape to the rabbet. Metal frames are not acidic and are, therefore, considered more appropriate for museum quality conservation.

Making a Simple Wooden Frame

Making your own frames can be most satisfying, not to mention economical. Frame making is a skill that requires careful attention to detail, because the success of any frame project relies on absolute accuracy. Frame making is a bit messy—there's the glue and sawdust—so keep your frame-making space separate from your mat cutting and frame-package assembling space. (When you're working with your art and glass and assembling your frame packages, cleanliness is of the utmost concern.) As with most endeavors, there are fancier, more expensive means available. However, to get started you can use some very basic inexpensive tools.

Tools and Materials

- **Wood moulding**—Make sure the rabbet of your moulding is deep enough to accommodate your frame package.

- **Ruler**

- **Pencil**

- **Miter box**—A device for making accurate 45° angle cuts that holds the moulding and has precise grooves for the tenon saw to ride in

- **Scrap wood**—This is placed in the miter box beneath your moulding to help the tenon saw leave a smoother edge. Use a piece 2 x 1 inches (5 x 2.5 cm).

- **Tenon saw**—A sturdy saw that's used with a miter box. This saw is very easy to control.

- **Fine-grain sandpaper**

- **Triangle or set square**—Used for checking the corners

- **Miter clamp**—Holds two pieces of moulding at a true 45° angle. This clamp is not required, but it provides some extra support while you're nailing.

- **Belt clamp**—Holds your entire frame at true angles, under tension, while the glue dries.

- **Glue**—White PVA wood glue. This is used to bond the mitered corners.

- **Pins**—Moulding or veneer pins are the kind of nails that are used (in conjunction with glue) to join the mitered corners.

- **Hammer**—Use a light to medium-weight hammer.

- **Nail set**—Used to countersink the nails

- **Clamps**—Used for securing your miter box to your tabletop, or to secure your molding to your table top.

Setting up Your Space

You want to create a very stable surface and minimize any wobble or unsteadiness with either your materials or your tools. You will enjoy more accurate cutting if things aren't shifting around. If you can, secure your miter box to your bench or table with clamps. If that's not workable, try clamping your molding to the table. This will help reduce excess movement while you saw. To this end, if you have an 8-foot (2.4 cm) piece of moulding, you may want to cut it down into pieces that are more manageable. (It's true—this is a bit wasteful, but it can make life a lot easier.) Have all of the things you'll need at the ready.

There are three distinct stages of frame making—measuring, cutting, and joining.

Measuring

First, you need to determine how much moulding you need to make your frame. To figure this, add the height and the width of your artwork package and multiply by two. This is the perimeter of your mounted picture. A sawing allowance must be added to the perimeter. To determine your sawing allowance, multiply the *width* of your moulding by eight. The sawing allowance plus the perimeter is the minimum length of moulding you need to make your frame. Now that we know how much moulding is required for our frame, we need to determine how long to cut each of the four sides.

We cut our moulding based on the measurements of the package (the glass, mat, art, mount, and backing). In our photo demonstration, our package is 8 x 10 inches (20 x 25 cm). Therefore, it would make sense that we need two short pieces of moulding cut to 8 inches (20 cm) and two long pieces cut to 10 inches (25 cm). However, to allow for a comfortable fit in the rabbet, we need to add 1/8 inch (3 mm) to each piece. Don't forget to add this extra to your measurements. To be on the safe side, always measure and mark twice. All your effort will be for naught if you fail to take the time now to measure properly.

Cutting

Put the moulding in the miter box face up and the rabbet side toward you. Keep a firm grip on your moulding. To get started, for the first few strokes just *pull* the saw back toward you. Then, *push* the saw to deepen the cut. Don't use much force. Let the weight of the saw do most of the work. Use steady smooth strokes.

1. Make a left-hand cut (photo 1) at one end of your moulding.

2. Measure and mark your first (longer piece) length on the rabbet from the cut you just made

(photo 2). Transfer this mark to the face of the moulding directly above the rabbet.

3. Make a right-hand cut precisely at the mark you made in step 2 (photo 3). This completes your first piece.

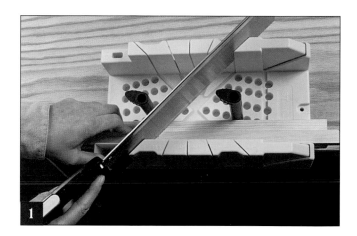

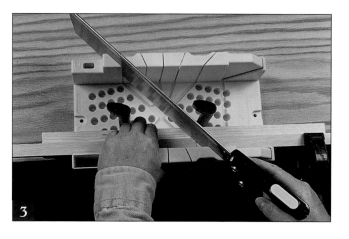

4

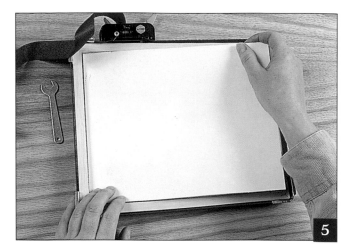

5

4. Repeat steps 1, 2, and 3. This completes your second piece. You have now cut the two long pieces of your frame.

5. Double-check your measurements and cuts. (Since you've cut the longer pieces first, if you've made a mistake you could turn these into your shorter pieces, if needed.)

6. Repeat this process for the two shorter pieces.

Joining

Before we get to the business of actually joining, let's check our corners with a triangle (photo 4). It may seem like a bother, but it's a good idea to clamp the frame together now to test for accuracy and fit. If we need to make any adjustments, the time is now, *before* we glue it up. Put your frame pieces together in the belt clamp and tighten until snug and even. Set your frame package into the rabbet (photo 5) and make sure the fit is good. If you've erred in measuring or have a bad cut, you'll need to identify the problem and fix it before moving forward.

1. Apply a small dab of glue to the ends of the frame and set back into place in the band clamp. Tighten the band (photo 6).

2. Wipe off any excess glue and allow the frame to dry completely (photo 7).

3. Once the frame is dry, we can nail the corners to give them additional support. Use the miter clamp (to brace corners), and lightly hammer in a moulding pin at each corner (photo 8). Larger frames may require several pins at each corner.

4. Use the nail set to lightly countersink the nails (photo 9).

6

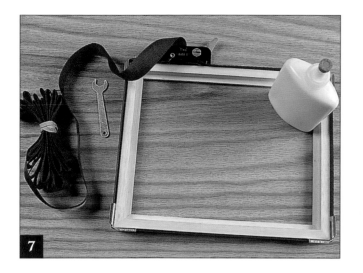

Assembling a Wooden Frame with Thumbnails

If the idea of putting a frame together appeals to you, but you don't want to build it from scratch, why not assemble a thumbnailed frame? You can have your choice of moulding custom cut (*chopped*) to your specifications. The ends of the moulding are routed. Plastic inserts, called *thumbnails* (photo 10) are used to join the routed pieces together. It's quite simple. (Packaged thumbnailed sectional frames are now available in craft and hobby stores.)

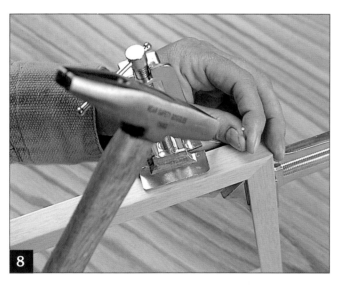

Tools and Materials

- Custom-chopped routed moulding
- PVA wood glue
- Clean rag
- Thumbnail inserts
- Rubber or plastic mallet

1. Lay out your frame moulding as shown.

2. Apply a small dab of glue to two ends (photo 11). Use a cotton swab to keep things tidy.

3. Insert a thumbnail into the routed corner (photo 12) and push it firmly into place.

4. If you meet considerable resistance, you may use a rubber or plastic mallet (not a hammer) to gently coax the thumbnail into place (photo 13).

5. Repeat steps 2, 3, and 4 with the other three corners.

6. Wipe off all the excess glue and allow the frame to dry (photo 14).

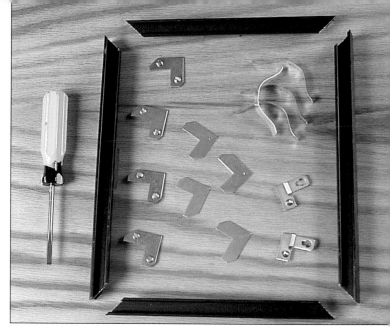

Assembling a Metal Sectional Frame

Perhaps you prefer the sleek, clean look of a metal frame. Why not purchase a sectional frame and assemble it yourself? Sectionals are sold in pairs—one pair for length and one for width. You can purchase them precut in packages, or have the moulding cut to your specifications. A metal sectional frame has a channel in the back of it where the joining hardware is inserted and tightened to secure the corners. Figure 5 shows a cross-sectional view of a typical metal sectional.

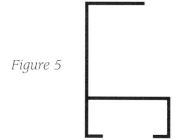

Figure 5

Tools and Materials

- Metal sectional frame
- Sectional hardware package
- Screwdriver

1. Lay out the tools and materials as shown.

2. Pair up the four corner plates—combine one set screw plate with one plain plate.

3. Put one corner plate into the channel at each end of the bottom section of the frame.

4. Slide the left and right sides onto the plates as shown in (photo15). Make the screws finger tight.

5. Insert a hanger into the left and right side channels. Leave finger tight.

6. Insert your frame package into the rabbet (photo 16).

7. Put a corner plate onto either end of the top section and slide the top down onto the sides. Make sure corners are flush (examine the front of the frame) and tighten all the screws. Tighten the

hangers in the desired position (Use metal spacers if the rabbet is too deep for your package).

8. Your frame is now ready to have the wire attached and be hung (photo 17).

Glazing

Regular/clear float glass and *low-iron glass* are the two types of glass commonly used for picture framing. Low-iron glass has less of a green tint than regular glass. Both are available in $3/32$-inch (2.4 mm) single strength and $1/8$-inch (3 mm) double strength. Several enhancements or filterings are available which reduce reflections, glare, and protect against UV rays. Nonglare and nonreflective enhancements definitely minimize the offending light play that can so often spoil the aesthetic pleasure of your framed art.

The glass is actually lightly etched with acid to make it slightly rough and opaque, which reduces its clarity. Generally, this decrease in clarity only becomes noticeable when the depth between the glass and art is increased. For example, triple-matted pictures will appear a bit soft. In addition, if you have a picture that isn't sharply defined to begin with, this extra blur may be too much. (Avoid acid etched glass if you're using conservation framing methods and products.) When considering what type of glass to use, consult with your local framer, know how your picture will be matted, and where it will be hung. If you know the lighting involved, you can better determine your glazing needs.

Professional framers recommend that you disassemble your framed package every five years and clean the inside of the glass. Inspect your picture and the rest of the elements of your frame package, as well. If you're going to be handling glass a lot, you can eliminate the mess from fingerprints and the natural oils from your

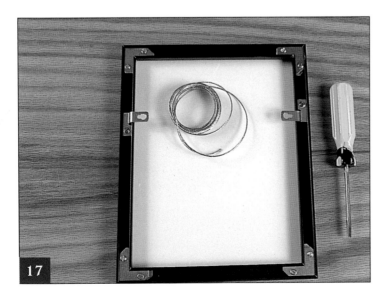

hands by wearing cotton gloves. Be careful to keep a tight hold on the glass. Keep the outside of the glass clean with spray glass cleaner and a soft cloth. Be conservative with the amount of cleaner you use, and never spray it directly on the glass—just spray the cloth. If it seeps under the glass, cleaner can stain your mat and wreck your artwork.

You may find it beneficial to use acrylic glazing, rather than glass. Let's take a look at some of the features and benefits of acrylic.

Weight: *Frame grade* (also referred to as .118 or ⅛ inch) acrylic is super lightweight. This acrylic has virtually all the nutrition, but only half the fat of regular glass. If you want to frame a large poster or oversized print, or if you frequently transport or handle your artwork, lightweight acrylic may be the way to go.

Strength: Compared to single strength glass, acrylic is a glutton for punishment. It's 30 times less likely to break, and if it does break, it will only crack. It will never shatter. (Hmm...do you have kids around?)

Enhancements: Acrylic glazing is available with all the popular enhancements of glass, including nonglare, UV-filtered, and nonabrasive. (Nonglare acrylic is roughed mechanically, not etched with acid.) Frame grade acrylic will not yellow the way other plastic products do.

On the down side, acrylic is notoriously easy to scratch. For this reason, special care must be taken when cleaning and handling. Acrylic should *only* be cleaned with a soft cloth and a product specifically designed for the purpose. Acrylic has a tendency to build up static electricity, so it is not recommended for framing charcoal, pastels, crayon, or any other friable media. Cutting acrylic is not a do-it-yourself activity, so you'll have to buy it precut or have it cut to size. Luckily, we can cut our own glass.

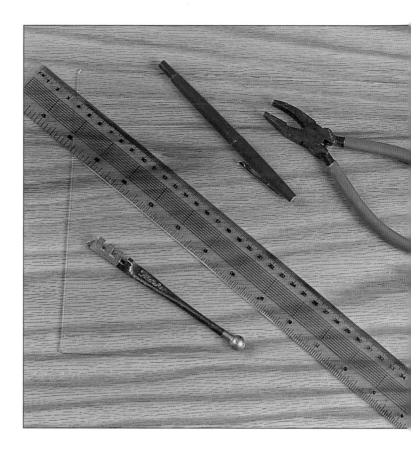

Cutting Glass

Tools and Materials

- Single-strength glass
- Ruler
- Fine-line marker, crayon, or grease pencil
- Glass cutter
- Glass-cutting pliers
- Soft clean cloth
- Glass cleaner (non-ammonia type)

Cutting your own glass is a skill well worth honing. It doesn't require much of an investment in tools or materials, but it does require the three P's—patience, practice, and perseverance. The most important thing to remember about cutting glass is that it is accomplished in two steps. The first step involves *etching* or *scoring* a line in the glass. The second step involves cleanly breaking the glass along the score line.

You need a smooth, flat surface on which to work. If you don't have a workbench (and have to use the kitchen table), make sure you protect your work surface with a piece of heavy cardboard or similar material. (Glass has a way of breaking when you don't want it to and not breaking when you do.) Until you're confident with your glass-cutting ability, make sure you have plenty of scrap with which to practice.

Glass cutters are such inexpensive tools that they're considered disposable, so when the wheel gets dull, toss it. You can prolong the life of your cutter by keeping the wheel-end immersed in kerosene (which prevents rusting) and occasionally oiling the wheel axle. Cutters should always be *wet* when used. Scoring with a *dry* tool creates a ragged, chipped score line. Built-in oil reservoirs are featured on some cutters to provide automatic wet cuts.

1. Using your pen and ruler, draw your cutting lines on the glass (photo 18). Make use of the existing outer edges whenever possible. (Remember you're cutting the glass the same size as your mat, mount, and backing. This measure-

ment should be within 1/16 inch [1.5 mm] of the rabbet size.)

2. Hold the ruler/straightedge along the line to be cut and place the glass cutter alongside it, perpendicular to the glass (photo 19). Start in about 1/8 inch (3 mm) from the edge of the glass. Using firm pressure, pull the cutter toward yourself with one slow, continuous stroke. Use a little less pressure as you end your stroke. (To successfully score the glass, it's imperative that you keep the wheel perpendicular and pull the cutter toward you with one fluid, firm motion. Do not stop and start.) You are simply scoring the glass, not trying to cut through it.

3. Place the scored glass along the edge of your table. Match up the scored line with the sharp edge of the table. (Keep the scored side facing up.)

4. Keep the glass on the table weighted with one hand (photo 20). With your other hand, hold the overhanging glass firmly. Raise it just slightly off the table, then snap it against the table edge.

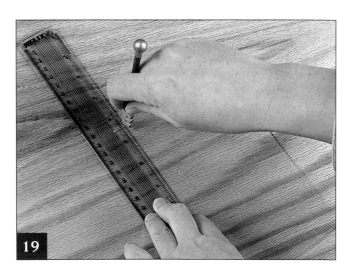

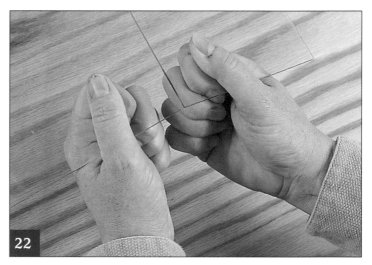

5. An alternative way of breaking the glass is with the help of a pair of glass-cutting pliers (photo 21). Hold the glass firmly on one side of the scored line. Hold the pliers in your other hand with the flat side on top. Open the pliers and grasp the glass near the scored line. Bend the pliers downward.

6. Another method of breaking the glass is to hold it close to the score line (photo 22). Roll your wrists inward, applying even upward pressure against the glass with both hands until it snaps. (Wear safety glasses during all scoring and breaking procedures.)

7. Run the toothed part of your cutter around the cut edges to get rid of any shards.

Although it might be tempting, do not run the glass cutter back over a scored line. This dulls the wheel and could shatter the glass. If you don't experience success on your first attempt, tap along the score line with the rounded end of your glass cutter and try to break it again.

Mats

Mat board consists of a paper face, a core, and a paper backing (figure 6). When the mat board is cut, the interior portion or core is exposed. The core is usually white or slightly brownish, but black and solid color cores are becoming increasingly popular. Mat board is most readily available in 4-ply thickness. A thick mat (8-ply) will provide a window twice as deep and create a more dramatic presentation for the artwork. Mat board is available precut or in large sheets. (See page 44 and 45 for more information on standard sizes.)

What Kind of Mat to Use

We talked a bit in the introduction about conservation quality products, techniques, and protection requirements. When you want to frame something that doesn't have real significant monetary value, it's certainly appropriate to get the least expensive mat available. However, for an original signed piece of fiber art or limited edition etching, you'll want a mat made to the highest standards. A good rule of thumb—for original and limited edition artwork use museum-quality mat. For ordinary works that you don't consider precious (craft projects, posters, home

decorating, non-original photos, etc.) neutralized mat will work just fine. For temporary pieces use the regular stuff.

Let's review the different types of mat board available:

Standard or regular mat Is made from ordinary wood pulp. The core of this board is slightly brownish. This board is acidic and should be used only with temporary works, not valuable works. This board does not offer indefinite protection and isn't conservation quality.

Neutralized mat Made from *buffered* wood pulp. This buffering slows the process of deterioration by temporarily neutralizing the acid in the wood pulp. Neutralized mat will last a very long time, but it is not totally acid free.

Rag mat or museum board Made from 100 percent cotton, with extra buffering to protect it from environmental contaminants. This board is acid-free and meets the Library of Congress standards for museum quality.

Alpha cellulose mat Made from wood pulp that has been processed to eliminate all acid-producing agents. This board is acid free and meets the Library of Congress standards for museum quality. (Note: A special *non-buffered* rag board is available that should be used for albumen, dye transfer, and chromogenic prints, and for silk and wood textiles.)

How to Choose a Mat

A huge array of colors and a variety of textures are available in both acid-free and conservation quality from your local frame shop. The larger mat board manufacturers sell swatch kits that contain corner samples (actual pieces of mat board for accurate color) of their boards

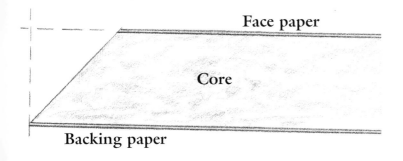

Face paper

Core

Backing paper

Figure 6

(photo 23). If you're doing a lot of matting, this is a great investment. You can coordinate all the available mat colors with your artwork and your home decor.

If you don't get a sample kit, take your artwork or photograph to the frame shop with you. To choose the most becoming color and texture, you need to have the artwork right up next to the mat. There is a dizzying array from which to choose. Experiment with different colors and color combinations, and ask your framer for suggestions. Remember that your objective is to

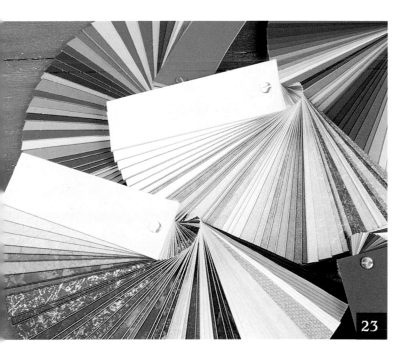

draw attention to the artwork and not to the mat. One of the easiest ways to accomplish this is to choose a mat that has the same or very similar color and value as a predominant color in the artwork (photo 24). Pairing a mat with the same color and value (lightness or darkness) as a predominant color in the artwork makes the mat blend in. If you choose a mat with a lighter value, there will be more contrast and the artwork will appear more pronounced. So too, if you choose a mat with a darker value than the artwork, the art

will be less pronounced. Look at your artwork...which colors are the most pronounced? Which colors are used the most?

When considering double or multiple mats, remember that artwork appears *more* prominent when the top mat is lighter than the bottom mats. Conversely, artwork will appear *less* prominent when your matting goes from dark to light. In most instances, the darker the mat, the closer it should be to the art.

Tips

■ Photos stand out with medium and pale-toned mat. ■ If you are framing a watercolor, keep in mind that white is rarely suitable. It flattens the picture and tends to make it appear darker. ■ To create a unified grouping of pictures, choose mats that are either all the same color or just subtle shades apart. ■ Oil paintings should never be matted. ■ A large mat can make a small picture look more important. ■ A small mat can make a large picture look more important.

Embellishing Mat Board

With such an overwhelming variety of mat board available, there doesn't seem to be much reason to embellish it yourself, unless you're cutting your own mat—in which case you're bound to end up with damaged and dinged pieces. Instead of throwing this "scrap" out, why not try some creative embellishment.

Blemished, severely overcut, dented, marred, scratched, or otherwise damaged mat board can be made new again with creative embellishments using a variety of media including: rubber-stamping, stenciled designs, sponge and spatter paint. Rub-on transfers can add subtle accents to mat corners. You can also purchase decorative adhesive tapes to mask trouble spots and create faux double mats. For stained or overcut boards, try wrapping them with fabric such as burlap, linen, silk, ultra suede, or hemp. Marbled and handmade papers make attractive covers, as does some embossed wallpaper. Turn a glaring scratch into a freehand carved design.

It should be noted that it takes very little to distract the eye from a picture. Mat board doesn't really need anything added to it, but sometimes you can get more mileage from your mat with just a little bit of embellishment. Remember that when it comes to embellishing mats, *less* is definitely *more*.

Making a Mat

The *mat window* or *cutout* (the opening through which your artwork is seen) is made with 45° beveled edges. The tool that creates these edges is called a *mat cutter*. Cutting your own mat board can be tremendously rewarding. However, before you pick up a mat cutter, it's vital to know how to measure your materials—success in mat cutting depends on accuracy in measuring. Precision is the key to mastering this exacting skill, and as every crafter knows, precision requires practice, patience, and perseverance. Let's take a look at what's required to get started.

Where to work: You'll need a clean, well-lit work space that's flat and stable. Mat cutting should be done standing up, with your materials at waist level. Adjust your work surface to accommodate your height, or stand on something sturdy to get the proper angle. Mat board should be handled with care. Dings and mars do have a way of magically appearing. If you're going to handle a lot of mat, consider wearing disposable surgical gloves. Fingerprints aren't a big problem, but the oils from your hands can really mess up certain boards. To minimize damage and protect your investment, keep your mat covered and laying flat. (You can keep it stored vertically, but only if it doesn't bend.) A whisk broom and a can of compressed air will help you keep things tidy. And unless you really like living on the edge, snacks and beverages should be banned from your work space.

Tools and Materials

There aren't that many tools required for cutting your own mats, but it is imperative to have quality tools. You'll be working with precise measurements, sharp blades, and costly materials, so don't skimp on your tools. Having said that, let me also add that it's a good idea to keep your initial investment conservative. You don't need to have the fanciest tools on the market (and there are plenty). I know folks who still use the same hand-held mat cutters they learned with years ago, and they wouldn't trade them for anything.

- **Mat cutter**—There are many different kinds of mat cutters available. From very basic hand-held models to very expensive, board-mounted, complex cutting systems. Start with a simple hand-held retractable blade cutter that you pull (not push) to cut. (You can buy an adapter that fits on your mat cutter and allows it to hook onto your straight edge-this is used in the photo demonstration.

It's a good idea for beginners and will make your cutting easier.)

- **Mat knife**—This is used for making straight cuts in mat.

- **Craft knife**—This comes in handy for detail work, like finishing undercuts.

- **Replacement blades**—Always have new blades on hand, and change your blade at the slightest suggestion of dullness-the sharper the better.

- **Metal straightedge**—A ruled nonskid cork or rubber base can save you a lot of mis-cutting. If you plan to use full sheets of mat board, get a 3-foot (1 m) straightedge. Make sure your straightedge is thick enough so that your mat cutter can't ride up over it.

- **Ruler**—A see-through, beveled edge type with inches and centimeters will be most useful.

- **HB or mechanical pencil**—Keep it very sharp. When you're first getting started, get in the habit of recording the dimensions on the wrong side of your mat board. It's easy to get confused with all the measurements, so write them down.

- **Mat board**—Don't skimp on your mat board. For most projects, you'll want quality acid-free board. Do get in the habit of saving your scraps-you never know when a strip or small piece will come in handy.

- **Cutting board**—A self-healing cutting base works very nicely. You can also use scrap or damaged mat or a soft wood board. You only have two hands-use clamps to keep your straightedge firmly in place, while you're cut ting the mat. This makes the process much easier and more enjoyable.

- **Burnishing tool**—This is used to smooth over cuts, and yes, you will make overcuts. You can buy a special tool, but try using the plastic-coated end of your mat knife first.

- **Tape measure**—If you prefer a tape measure to a ruler, use a lightweight cloth tape measure. It is less likely to damage artwork and mat board, if you drop it.

When we consider mat board measurements, it's in relation to the picture we wish to frame and the frame we'll put the picture in. This is an important consideration. We need to keep the artwork or picture and the frame in mind, before we cut our mat. It's also important to note that in picture framing there are *standard* sizes and *custom* sizes.

Let's say you find a wonderful print, and you buy a great-looking mat board that looks stunning with it. You cut a perfect window for your print and make 3½-inch boarders (8.8 cm) on all sides. Then you go to buy a frame and discover that your matted masterpiece is not a *standard* size, so you have to order a *custom-made* frame, which will cost a small fortune and, of course, it won't be ready until your toddler's off to college. You see, you can't cut mat in a vacuum; it is part of the bigger framing picture. Please review the Standard Sizes chart on page 43 before you start cutting. You may certainly cut your mat whatever size you wish, as long as you realize that precut glass and ready–made frames are only available in certain sizes.

First, let's commit these measuring mantras to memory:

Always read your ruler from above, not from an angle.

Measure twice. Cut once.

Always check your corners with a set square, triangle, or protractor.

All measurements and cuts are made on the back or *wrong* side of the mat.

Measuring

1. First, we need to determine the size of the mat *window*. The window refers to the cutout in the mat through which your artwork will show. In order to know what size to cut your window, you need to know the size of your picture. So, first measure your picture. In figure 7, the size of the picture is 8 x 10 inches (20.3 x 25.4 cm). Most often, you'll want the mat to just overlap your picture. To ensure that your picture will not slip through the window, make your opening a minimum of ⅛ inch (3 mm) smaller than the picture, on all sides. Figure 8 shows the size of the mat window, which is 7¾ x 9¾ inches (19.68 x 24.7 cm). Notice we've subtracted ¼-inch (6 mm) from the width and ¼ inch (6 mm) from the height of our picture. This provides the ⅛-inch (3 mm) overlap we need on all sides. (Note: if there is an artist's signature, plate mark, or numbered edition notation, you'll want to leave extra [white] space between your image and your mat—1 to 2 inches [2.5 to 5 cm] is customary. For balance, this allowance should be continued all around, but it can be narrower on the top and sides.)

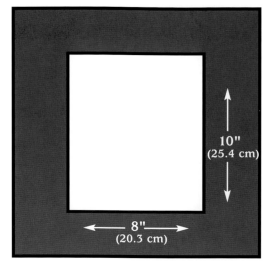

Figure 7

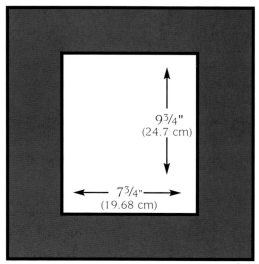

Figure 8

2. The next step is to determine the size of the mat borders. Figure 9 shows 2⅛ inch (5.4 cm) mat borders all around. There is no magic formula for calculating exactly how wide your mat borders should be. Average borders are between 2 and 4 inches (5 and 10 cm) with 3 inches (7.5 cm) considered *standard* in the framing business. Often, the bottom border is cut slightly larger than the top and sides. In *framespeak*, this is referred to as *offsetting* or *weighing the mat*. Offsetting compensates for the natural optical illusion of top-heaviness that exists. We actually see equally cut borders as being larger on top.

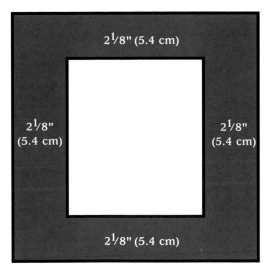

Figure 9

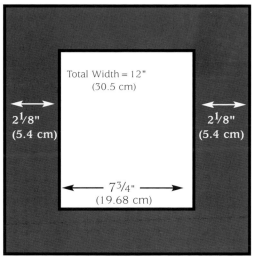

Figure 10

When the mat is weighted, the eye is fooled into perceiving balance. This is very subtle, but it makes for a more agreeable presentation. (The bottom border may be cut even larger to help a square boxy print look more pleasingly rectangular.) Borders are usually cut at least twice as wide as the moulding, and for frames larger than 20 x 24 inches (50 x 60 cm), the borders should be at least three times as wide. The bottom line is to make your borders wide enough so that your picture is clearly separated from the edge of your frame. When in doubt, go wider.

3. Now we can determine the outside dimension or the overall size of the mat board. Add the mat **window** dimensions (that you figured in step 1) to the mat **border** dimensions (that you figured in step 2). This gives us the outside dimension of our mat board or the total mat size. Figures 10 and 11 show the calculations for the outside dimension. This outside dimension will be the same size as the frame, glass, and backing. Now we can proceed to the cutting stage.

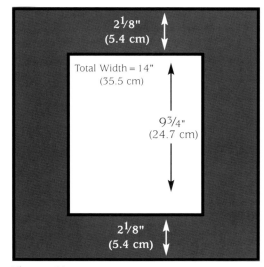

Figure 11

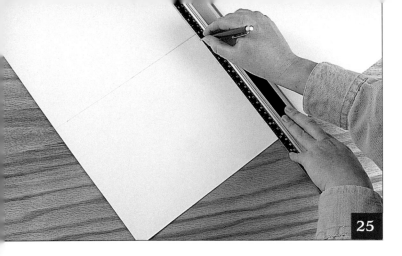

25

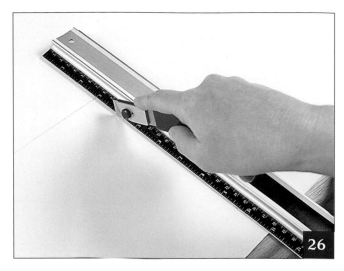

26

Cutting

1. First, we'll transfer the outside dimension measurements onto the back of the mat board (photo 25). Use a sharp pencil and ruler, and start at a corner of your mat board to minimize waste. (Check that your corner is 90°true with a triangle or protractor.)

2. Use your mat knife and ruler/straightedge to cut the mat along the lines you've made (photo 26). This is a critical stage because if you don't have four perfect 90° corners, each subsequent cut you make will be off just enough to drive you crazy when you assemble your frame package.

3. Next, we'll transfer the window opening dimensions onto the back of the mat. Mark your window with a sharp pencil, and cross your lines at the corners (photo 27). Recheck your border measurements.

4. Position your straightedge along the outside of the drawn line and firmly hold in place. Clamping your straightedge in position can be a great help. It allows you to focus more on cutting and use less physical energy doing it (photo 28).

5. Place your mat cutter against the straightedge. Hook it onto the straightedge if you've attached an adapter (photo 29). Push the blade into the mat at the appropriate starting point and pull the cutter smoothly along the straightedge, stopping at the corner mark. Retract the blade,

27

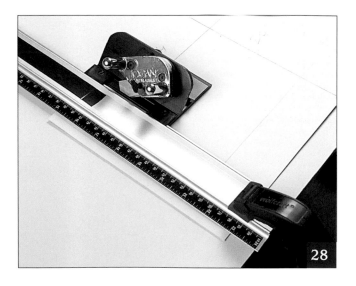

28

turn the board clockwise, reposition, and repeat the process until all the sides have been cut. (If the mat cutter is difficult to pull, the blade may be dull or it may be set to cut too deep. Put in a new blade, or reset the blade so it just cuts through the mat, but barely scratches the cutting board.)

6. The center should now *fall out* leaving you with a perfectly cut mat window (photo 30). If you are human and live in the real world, chances are your corners will be slightly undercut. Use a craft knife with a very sharp blade to finish the job (photo 31).

7. For overcut corners, a burnishing tool applied to the front of the board will minimize the appearance (photo 32).

Once you're comfortable with the basics of mat measuring and cutting, why not try your hand at other types of decorative cuts-offset corners, V-grooves, ovals, and freehand cutting. Contemporary creative matting is a real art form. Visit your local frame shop to get more ideas and see if they offer classes in more sophisticated mat cutting techniques. Also, start paying attention to the way things are matted; but remember many professionals now use computerized mat cutting systems, so don't feel bad if your work doesn't quite measure up to theirs.

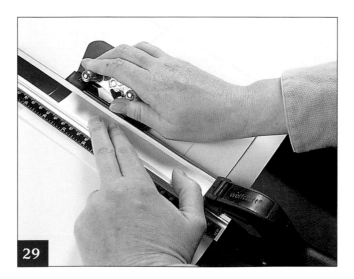

Mounts

Mounting is the process of attaching your picture or artwork to a firm support board in order to keep it secure and prevent it from rippling. This process is especially important because your picture is in *direct contact* with the mount board, and this exposes your picture to potential damage.

In the good old days, if you had a family photograph or picture you wanted to mount, you probably reached for some cellophane or masking tape, a discarded cardboard box, and the scissors. Well, the care and preservation of paper art has come a long way and today those old do-it-yourself standbys are regarded as downright deplorable. We now know that the adhesives in many tapes are actually quite corrosive. The wrong tapes can become brittle over time, leave nasty residues, and turn your favorite photos yellow. Regular old cardboard will degrade paper art over time, as well. There's a lot to consider: acidity, pH balance, moisture, calcium carbonate buffering, alkaline reserve, atmospheric acid contamination, and chemical adhesive reactions. Happily, you can avoid the ruinous acid-burn of yesteryear without being a chemist.

A variety of techniques and products are available to help protect our cherished keepsakes. When considering which mounting technique and materials to use, you must take into account the *value* of what you're framing. As discussed in the introduction, not everything you frame will warrant museum-quality standards. If you're working with something of little monetary or sentimental value (and you really don't care if it lasts 100 years), you can stick with double-sided tape to adhere your item directly to the mount board. If you are moderately concerned with conservation and want to provide solid protection to your artwork, you can safely mount your work using all acid-free materials. If you want the highest level of protection available and the ability to remove your artwork from its mount in the future (called *reversibility*), you need archival-standard techniques, and you should consult a professional framer who specializes in such. Decide what is

appropriate for you based on your particular artwork and your style of matting.

If you have extremely valuable or fragile artwork, you'll want to consider a visit with your local framer. He or she has the special equipment and expertise you need for a professional job. Having said that, if your art is of a more casual interest, you can do a fine job yourself if you follow some basic guidelines.

A variety of suitable boards are available for mounting artwork, including:

- Museum-quality (4-ply) mat board

- Foam core (acid-free)

- Regular mount board (acid-free)

- Corrugated cardboard (acid-free)

- Premium-grade news board

- Self-adhesive mount board

- Illustration board

- Poster board

In most instances, use either the museum-quality or foam boards. If you have an impermanent, budget-driven project, an inexpensive poster board will work just fine. (Note: To mount anything larger than 16 x 20 inches [40 x 50 cm], use a heavyweight board such as 3/16-inch [5 mm] foam core or a 3X type mount board.)

Let's take a look at some mounting techniques:

Mounting with Paper Hinges

This archival technique uses torn (not cut) strips of Japanese rice papers as hinges and cooked rice or wheat starch pastes as adhesives. This museum-quality method is completely *reversible*, meaning the artwork can be removed from the mount without changing it—no glue is left on it and no fibers have been pulled from it. Leave this procedure to the professional framer who specializes in archival framing techniques.

Mounting with Corners and Strips

If you had a photo album or scrapbook when you were a kid, I'll bet you remember those old paper photo corners that you had to lick to stick. Well, here's a kinder, gentler version that will be perfect for most of your mounting jobs. These corners and strips are convenient to use, and they provide archival-quality protection for your work. (Make sure you use the archival-quality mounting corners and strips that are made of polyester film and are backed with acid-free adhesive that never directly contacts the art.) Use this method for overmatted artwork where the mat window is *smaller* than the picture. The corners or strips will be hidden from view. (Some works may not be rigid enough to be effectively mounted with corners or strips. If your picture or artwork is on the flimsy side, you might want to use the T-hinge method instead.)

Tools and Materials

- Mat board
- Mount board (foam core)
- Mounting corners (also called *pockets*) or strips
- Artwork
- Acid-free artist's tape or white linen tape
- Scissors
- Pencil

(Note: Cut your mount board the same size as your mat board.)

1. Hinge your window mat to your mount board by positioning the mat face down and the mount face up, with their edges together (photo 33).

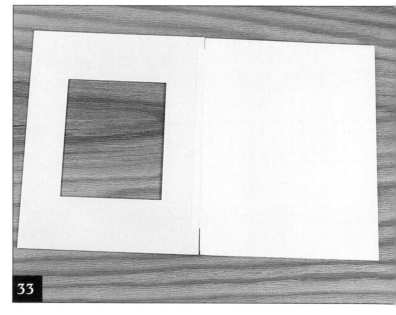

2. Tape the edges together using acid-free artist's tape or white linen tape (photos 34, 35). Leave an inch (2.5 cm) at either end untaped. Close the mat and make sure the corners are properly aligned.

3. Position your picture on the mount board (photo 36). Make sure you get your picture exactly where you want it. Close the mat and check that your positioning is right. Carefully mark the corners on the mount board.

4. Attach the four mounting corners a bit beyond the corners you just marked on the mount board.

It's extremely important that you allow a little extra breathing room at each corner.

5. Position your picture in the corners and close the mat (photo 37).

(Note: Corners are available in different sizes—from small to extra large. Make sure the mounting corners you use are the correct size to accommodate the weight and size of your picture or artwork. For pictures larger than 11 x 14 inches [27.5 x 35 cm], use the extra large corners.)

Mounting strips are used in much the same way as corners, except they hold your artwork in place from all four *sides*. Mark the *outline* of your picture (instead of the corners) and attach the strips (the outer half has an adhesive backing) at the marks. Insert your picture under the strips to secure.

Mounting with T-Hinges

Follow steps 1 through 3 as described in Mounting with Corners, then:

1. Attach two pieces of tape to the back of your picture as shown in photo 38.

2. Reposition your picture on the mount board and attach two more pieces of tape over the sticky hinges you just attached (photo 39). (The pieces of tape form the letter T, thus the name.)

3. Close the mat.

Mounting with X-Hinges

This technique is used to *float* mount your picture or artwork. A mat window is not used, but an attractive piece of mat board is used as the mount. Since the entire picture is visible, the hinges are hidden on the back of the artwork. This is typically used with watercolors and attractive deckle (torn) edged papers.

1. Lightly mark the corner positions of your artwork on your mount board.

2. Use two pieces of artist's tape or linen tape and form the letter X. The adhesive sides are facing each other (figure11).

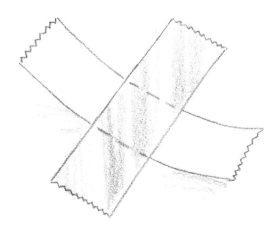

Figure 11

3. Place two X-hinges onto the back of your picture near the top corners (figure 12). (If you have a large picture, use three hinges.)

4. Position your picture on the mount board and press to adhere (figure 13).

Figure 12

Figure 13

Permanent Mounting

This type of mounting works well with posters, maps, illustrations, greeting card/calendar graphics, some photos, digital and copier papers, postcards, newsprint, etc. *Permanent* is the operative word here, because once you've bonded the picture to the mount board, the two shall never part. While this type of mounting is quite convenient for items of casual interest, do not consider it an option for precious or valuable works. Generally the mount board is cut the same size as the picture and often no mat is used. Instead, spacers are used to create an air cushion between the glass and art. Often, works that have been permanently mounted are additionally set in sink mounts before matting and framing. (See page 39 for sink mount instructions.)

Here are several permanent mounting options:

Spray adhesive: An aerosol adhesive product is applied directly to the mount board and allowed to dry to a light tack. The picture is then placed on the board, and pressure is evenly applied (you can use a rolling pin, brayer, or squeegee) to create the bond. Allow complete drying. Always use these products in well-ventilated areas, and don't overspray or you'll wind up with a big sticky mess. Be sure to follow the manufacturer's instructions and recommendations for substrate (mount board) compatibility. Work with extreme care to avoid wrinkles and air bubbles.

Self-adhesive foam core: One side of this board is coated with a layer of acid-free adhesive beneath a protective peel-off layer, or release liner. It's a lot less messy than the spray adhesives, and the adhesive coating is said to be "positionable," meaning you have some time to fine-tune the position of your picture without the stress of misalignment and the fear of premature adhesion. To use the self-stick board (also called "sticky board"), cut it to the size of your picture and peel back about 1 inch (2.5 cm) of the top of the release liner. Align your picture and lightly press it onto the exposed adhesive. Gradually remove the release liner, while pressing your picture into place. Allow your work to dry undisturbed for several hours before handling. (Note: If you're mounting a piece larger than 16 x 20 inches [40 x 50 cm] you'll want to adhere it from the *center* instead of the top edge. Score a line across the center of the board, and peel back the release liner about 1 inch [2.5 cm]. Align and press your picture as before, but work from the center to the bottom, then from the center to the top.)

This type of mounting board is available in both low and high tack. Both adhesive formulas are acid-free, but the high tack is better suited to needlework and fiber art. Remember that this process is not reversible. Think twice about mounting works of monetary or sentimental value this way.

Mounting Needlework

If you're like many stitchers I know, you have a drawerful of completed pieces that you just haven't gotten around to framing. Well, it's time to get your beautiful work up on the walls where it belongs! Framing your needlework isn't that difficult, but it does take some extra care. Fiber art requires just as much protection from acid burn as paper art does. Acidic materials will turn your fabrics yellow faster than you can say "a stitch in time saves nine," so make sure you use acid-free materials. Antique fabrics are often very valuable and extremely fragile. If you have antique needlework, please consult a professional picture framer who specializes in such.

Quick-Stick Mount

This is the quickest method to use by far. The edges of your needlework are attached to the (acid-free) adhesive back of the mount board as shown in figures 14 and 15. If you are concerned about future remounting, you can sew extra borders onto your work. These extra borders are

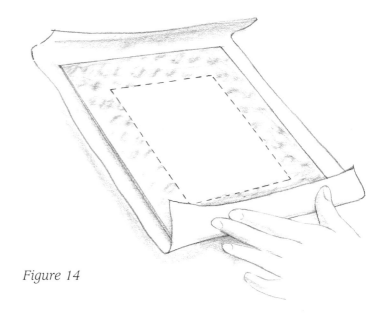

Figure 14

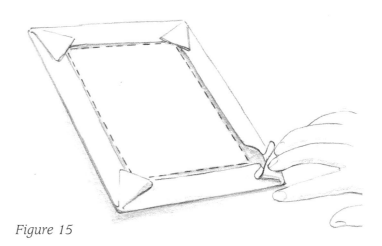

Figure 15

attached to the adhesive, instead of your original material, making removal easy and harmless.

Pinning

There are several ways to pin your work. If you are going to leave the pins in your work, you definitely will want to use stainless steel ballpoint pins. If you use the pins temporarily, regular T-pins are fine.

40

Tools and Materials

- Foam core (acid-free)
- T-pins
- Needle art
- Double-sided tape (acid-free)
- Scissors

1. Cut your foam core about 1 inch (2.5 cm) larger than your mat window.

2. Start at the top and pin your needlework into the center of the foam core. Work your way out to the corners (photo 40).

3. Keep your work stretched taut and centered as you pin. Keep your pins spaced about ½-inch (1.3 cm) apart.

4. When you've finished pinning, turn your work over and apply a length of double-sided tape along one edge.

5. Stretch the fabric across the taped area and smooth down (photo 41). Repeat on all sides.

6. Trim the excess material at each corner and secure with tape (photo 42).

7. Remove pins.

An alternative is to not use any adhesive and leave your pins in place. Stainless steel ballpoint pins (silk pins) are recommended for this option.

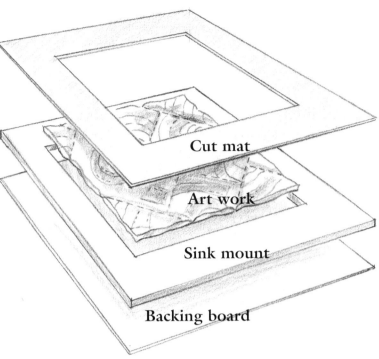

Figure 16

Sink Mounts

Once you have your needlework mounted to a support, you're ready to mat and frame it. Depending on your particular project, you might need to make a sink mount to allow you to mat it properly. A sink mount provides an extended support surface for securing your mat and backing (figure 16).

1. Cut a piece of foam core (the same thickness of your mounted work) the same size as the outside dimension of your mat board.

2. Cut a window in the foam core to accommodate your mounted needlework. Cut it just a hair larger to allow for expansion and contraction.

3. Hinge your mat to your sink mount (as described on page 33 and 34).

4. Insert your needlework, and frame the package.

As you proceed with your framing project, remember that your needlework should not come in direct contact with the glass. Therefore, if you've decided not to use a mat, you'll want to use *spacers* (clear plastics rods) instead. Spacers are put in place after the glass has been set in the frame. They form a vertical wall and create the necessary air cushion between your needlework and the glass. They're available (cut to size) from your local frame shop.

In the figure, the labels read:
Cut mat
Art work
Sink mount
Backing board

Putting It All Together

Now that you've selected your picture, made your frame, cut your mat and your glass, and mounted your picture, it's time to put it all together (figure 17).

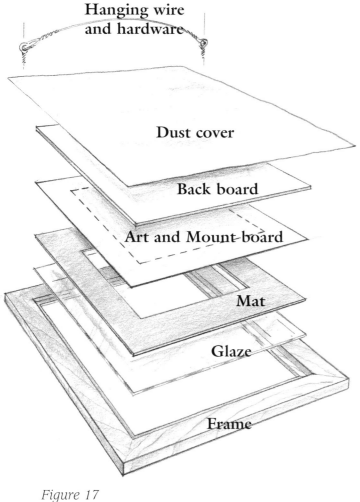

Hanging wire and hardware

Dust cover

Back board

Art and Mount board

Mat

Glaze

Frame

Figure 17

Tools and Materials

- Frame package (glass, mat, picture, mount board, and back board)
- Glazing points
- Point pusher
- PVA glue or double-sided tape
- Brown kraft paper
- Craft knife
- Ruler/straightedge
- Screw eyes or strap hangers
- Awl
- Wire
- Bumpers

3. Squeeze a bead of glue along the back of the frame. Spread smooth with a damp sponge as shown in photo 44. (You may use double-sided tape if you prefer.)

4. Cover the back of the frame with an oversized piece of kraft paper. Pull it taut and press it onto the glue (photo 45).

5. Use a ruler and craft knife to trim the paper to fit. Trim it to ⅛ inch (3 mm) inside the edges (photo 46).

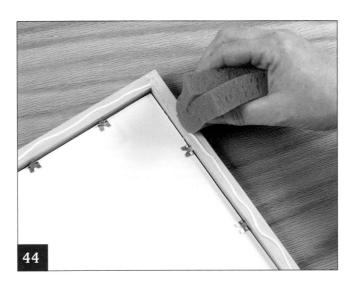

1. Put your frame package in your frame. (Give your glass one last cleaning before putting it in the frame. Make sure the inside of your frame is clean, too.)

2. Use the glazing points and the point pusher (or putty knife) as shown in photo 43 to secure the package in the frame. Push the points firmly into place. (You could also use small brads and a lightweight hammer for this.)

6. Attach the screw eyes about one-quarter the length of the frame from the top. Use the awl to start your holes, and twist the screws in (photo 47).

7. Insert the wire through one screw eye and wrap it back around itself four or five times. Stretch it across the frame and through the other screw eye. To make sure you don't get too much slack in the wire, use one of your fingers as a hanger. You don't want the wire to show from the front (photo 48). Once you get the position right, wrap the wire around itself at the other end.

8. Attach self-adhesive protective bumpers to the bottom corners of the frame (photo 49).

9. The picture is now finally ready to hang (photo 50).

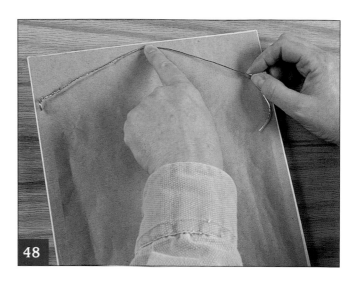

A Note on Standard Sizes

Frames, glazing, and precut mat board are readily available in standard sizes. These sizes are used because they are the most commonly needed for framing photographs. You may purchase materials with different dimensions, but you will pay more because they are usually considered custom.

Here are some sizes for the home crafter and do-it-yourselfer to keep in mind:

Remember that the frame size actually refers to the size of the rabbet. The rabbet is the recess into which your glass, mat, art, mount, and backing fit. The size of the rabbet is actually smaller than the outside dimensions of the frame.

Frame Sizes (Standard)

- 8 x 10 inches (20 x 25 cm)

- 11 x 14 inches (27.5 x 35 cm)

- 14 x 17 inches (35 x 42.5 cm)

- 14 x 18 inches (35 x 45 cm)

- 16 x 20 inches (40 x 50 cm)

- 20 x 24 inches (50 x 61 cm)

- 24 x 30 inches (62 x 76 cm)

Moulding Sizes

Frame moulding is available by length in 8- to 12-foot (2.4 to 3.6 m) pieces. You can have your local framer or chop shop cut it for you, or purchase it whole and cut it yourself. Length moulding is priced by the foot. Metal frames are often packaged in pairs of equal length. These pairs (called sectionals) are available in 1-inch (2.5 cm) increments and offer a convenient way for do-it-yourselfers to make their own custom-sized frames. (Assembly hardware is included with pre-packaged sectionals.) You can also have metal length molding cut or chopped to your specifications. (Hardware isn't generally included with custom-cut aluminum lengths.)

Artwork that is vertically oriented is referred to as portrait. Horizontally oriented artwork is called landscape.

Portrait

Landscape

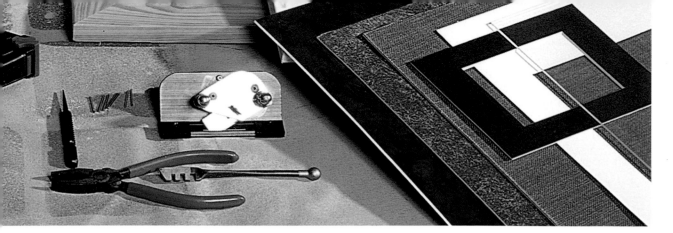

Mat Sizes

There are several ways to purchase mat board:

Full sheets: 32 x 40 inches (81 x 102 cm) or 40 x 60 inches (102 x 152 cm).

Standard-cut sheets (without windows): Refer to the mat size column in the chart.

Pre-cut (with standard-size window openings):

Sizes in inches

Mat Size	Window Size	Picture size	Borders
8 x 10	$4^{1}/_{2}$ x $6^{1}/_{2}$	5 x 7	$1^{3}/_{4}$
9 x 12	$5^{1}/_{2}$ x $7^{1}/_{2}$	6 x 8	$1^{3}/_{4}$
11 x 14	$7^{1}/_{2}$ x $9^{1}/_{2}$	8 x 10	$1^{3}/_{4}$
12 x 16	$8^{1}/_{2}$ x $11^{1}/_{2}$	9 x 12	$1^{3}/_{4}$
16 x 20	$10^{1}/_{2}$ x $13^{1}/_{2}$	11 x 14	$2^{3}/_{4}$
16 x 20	$11^{1}/_{2}$ x $15^{1}/_{2}$	12 x 16	$2^{1}/_{4}$
20 x 24	$15^{1}/_{2}$ x $19^{1}/_{2}$	16 x 20	$2^{1}/_{4}$
30 x 40	$19^{1}/_{2}$ x $23^{1}/_{2}$	20 x 24	$5^{1}/_{4}$

Sizes in centimeters

Mat Size	Window Size	Picture size	Borders
20 x 25	11.3 x 16.3	12.5 x 17.5	4.5
22.5 x 30	13.8 x 18.8	15 x 20	4.5
27.5 x 35	18.8 x 23.8	20 x 25	4.5
30 x 40	21.3 x 29.5	22.5 x 30	4.5
40 x 50	27 x 34.5	27.5 x 35	7
40 x 50	29.5 x 39.5	30 x 40	6
50 x 61	39.5 x 50	40 x 50	6
76 x 102	50 x 60.5	50 x 62	13.5

Mat and Mount Thickness

The thickness of a board is expressed in the # of layers (or plys) it has.

- 2-ply board is 1/32 inch (.75 mm) thick.

- 4-ply board is 1/16 inch (1.5 mm) thick (this is the standard for mat, which allows ample separation of artwork and glazing).

- 8-ply board is 1/8 inch (3 mm) thick. An 8-ply mat board provides a deep, dramatic window. An 8-ply mount board is frequently used for oversized artwork that requires extra support.

- 14-ply and 28-ply boards are used for heavy weight items and are referred to as X and 3X boards, respectively.

Foam Core Board

Standard sheets are 32 x 40 inches (81 x 102 cm) and are available in both 3/16 inch (5 mm) and 1/8 inch (3 mm). Oversize sheets are 48 x 96 inches (122 x 244 cm) and are available in 3/16 inch (5 mm).

Picture Framing Wire

Braided wire is sized according to the number of strands it has. The more strands the wire has, the greater the breaking strength. The rule of thumb is that your wire should be able to support four times the weight of your picture.

Number of Strands	Size	Breaking Strength
8	1	34
12	2	51
16	3	68
20	4	85
24	5	122

picture perfect projects

Faux Gild

Designed by Tammy Lou Grant

All that glitters is not gilded. If you love the look, but don't have the time or patience for traditional gilding, try this quick and easy technique.

Tools
- *Palette*
- *Sponge*
- *Paper towels*
- *Paintbrush*

Materials
- *8 x 10-inch (20 x 25 cm) picture frame*
- *Gold metallic spray paint*
- *Acrylic paint—red and black*

Instructions

1. Spray the frame with gold metallic paint. Allow to dry. (Apply two coats if needed.)

2. Pour a small amount of red paint onto a palette. Use a barely damp sponge and generously paint the frame. Make sure the paint gets into the corners.

3. While the red paint is still wet, use the paper towel to wipe it off. Leave on as much or as little of the red paint as you desire. Allow to dry.

4. Apply black paint with the paintbrush to the lip of the frame. Use the paper towel to wipe it off to achieve the desired effect. Allow to dry.

5. Repeat step 4 on the outer edge of the frame.

Note: You may use an ivory colored paint before applying the red. You may also re-spray the corners gold after step 3. Experiment until you find the color combination you desire.

Abacus Frame

Designed by Linda Rose Nall

You can count on this frame...for fun. This beaded wire extension frame is made from ordinary coat hangers that are soldered together.

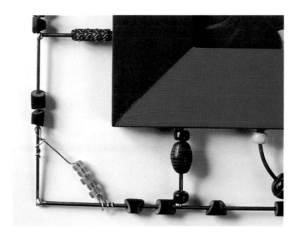

Tools
- *Ruler and pencil*
- *Drill with small bit*
- *Paintbrush*
- *Tin snips*
- *Silicon tube glue*
- *Soldering iron*
- *Flux and brush*
- *Solder (60/40 lead/tin mix)*
- *Very fine steel wool*
- *Wire cutters*
- *Round-nose pliers*

Materials
- *8 x 6¹/₂-inch (20 x 16.3 cm) wooden frame*
- *Acrylic paint—red and purple*
- *5 wire coat hangers*
- *Beads*
- *20-gauge wire—2 feet (60 cm) (optional)*

Instructions

1. Measure and mark three spots (equally spaced) on each edge of the frame.

2. Drill 12 holes where marked, ¹/₂ inch (1.3 cm) deep.

3. Paint the frame red and purple as shown. Use care to keep the holes free of paint.

4. Use the tin snips to cut 12 pieces of coat hanger into 2-inch (5 cm) lengths. (You can make eight of these pieces straight and four of them curved, if you wish.)

5. Glue the 12 pieces of coat hanger in the 12 holes. Stick each piece of wire in the tube of silicon glue, then insert in the holes. (The four curved pieces were used in the center holes on this frame.) Let the glue set overnight.

6. Add your choice of beads (coordinate color with frame) to the 12 pieces of wire.

7. Cut two pieces of wire hanger 10 inches (25 cm) each and two pieces 11¹/₂ inches (29 cm) each.

8. Line up the long pieces around the frame to form a square. Add beads to the long pieces, as desired.

9. Turn your soldering iron on.

10. Choose a side and brush flux onto the three wire ends. Hold the long wire piece in place and drop a bead of solder onto each of the three joints. Repeat this process with the other three sides of the frame.

11. Solder the four corners of the wire abacus.

12. Wash and rinse the joints with dish soap and very fine (0000) steel wool. Pat dry.

13. Optional: Cut four pieces of 20-gauge wire 6-inch (15 cm) lengths. String with beads and add to corners as shown. Wrap the ends securely in place using round-nose pliers.

Mosaic Mirror
Designed by Linda Rose Nall

This mosaic-framed mirror is big, bold, and fun to make. Mirrors provide a great opportunity to reflect your wildest expression of color. So, don't hold back.

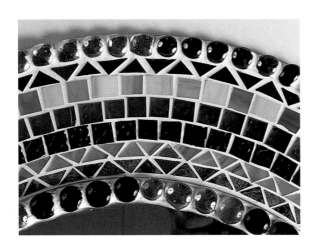

Tools
- *Silicon tube glue*
- *Putty knife or scraper*
- *Sponge*
- *Container of water*
- *Soft cloth*
- *Glass cleaner*

Materials
- *Mirror of your choice; 24-inch- diameter (60 cm) used here*
- *Different shapes and colors of glass tiles*
- *Different colors of glass blobs*
- *Premixed tile grout*

Instructions

1. Lay out the tiles and blobs on your mirror in the design you want. Leave about ¹/₈ inch (3 mm) between pieces for the grout.

2. Once you have determined your pattern, glue the pieces in place.

3. Allow the mirror to dry for 24 hours.

4. Apply the grout with the putty knife or scraper. You could also use a "grout float" available at your local hardware store. (Read and follow the grout manufacturer's instructions.)

5. Make sure the grout fills in between the tiles.

6. Let the grout set according to package instructions, and then wipe off the excess with the sponge. Use water to keep your sponge clean. Keep the sponge damp, but not soaked.

7. Wipe the surface down until it is clean, and allow it to set overnight.

8. If your grout has settled, you may need to reapply. If so, repeat steps 4 through 7.

9. To finish, wipe the tiles clean with a soft cloth and a bit of glass cleaner. Finally, clean the mirror.

Bamboo Frame

Designed by Travis Waldron

Spice up an ordinary frame with an exotic Far East flavor. Bamboo is easy to work with—it cuts like butter and barely adds any weight.

Tools
- *Paintbrush*
- *Clear acrylic spray*
- *Sharp pruners or shears*
- *Glue gun and glue sticks*

Materials
- *16 x 16-inch (40 x 40 cm) frame*
- *Acrylic paint—black and burgundy*
- *Bamboo*

The style of frame you use can influence how you add the bamboo. The frame used here has a wide raised lip and a scoop design. Using the smaller diameter bamboo on the inside and the larger along the outside edge worked well with this particular frame style. You might do the same, but feel free to experiment with your own frame and different bamboo patterns, until you find what pleases you most.

Instructions

1. Paint the face and inside edges of the frame black. Paint the outside edges of the frame burgundy. Allow to dry thoroughly.

2. Spray the frame with the clear acrylic spray. Allow to dry.

3. Heat your glue gun.

4. Cut one small stalk of bamboo so that one end is flush with the lip of the frame and the other end extends a ¼ inch (6 mm) beyond the lip.

5. Glue this piece into place, using your glue gun. Turn your frame 90°.

6. Measure your next piece of bamboo so that it butts up to the end of the first piece and extends ¼ inch (6 mm) beyond the lip on the other end. Glue this piece into place.

7. Repeat this process with two more pieces of bamboo. You have now completed the first "row."

8. The next row is made in the same way, except all pieces extend ¼ inch (6 mm) on each end. Make this row as close to the first one as possible.

9. Continue this way until you have covered the entire face of the frame.

Note: Since bamboo is not perfectly symmetrical, you may want to add some very thin pieces to cover any big gaps or hide any imperfections.

Leather Upholstery Frame

Designed by Travis Waldron

A scrap of leather and a handful of upholstery tacks transformed this plain plywood frame into a handsome accessory befitting the most elegant decor.

Tools

- *Felt-tipped or fabric marker*
- *Scissors*
- *Spray adhesive*
- *PVA craft glue*
- *Small hammer*

Materials

- *5 x 7-inch (12.5 x 17.5 cm) frame*
- *Leather scrap (to fit frame size)*
- *20 to 24 upholstery tacks*

Instructions

1. Lay your leather face down on a clean work surface. Place your frame on the fabric, and trace around the edges of the frame with a felt-tipped or fabric marker.

2. Now, add about 1 inch (2.5 cm) to your outside edge and 1 inch (2.5 cm) to your inside edge. (This extra is needed so you can wrap your leather around the frame. If you're using a particularly deep frame, you might want to add a little extra.) Cut around the outside edge of the leather and set it aside.

3. Spray the entire surface of your frame with adhesive. (Read and follow manufacturer's instructions.)

4. Lay the leather (face up) over the frame. Smooth any wrinkles or folds. Apply pressure, and allow the bond to set.

5. Turn the frame over and spray adhesive along the back and sides. Carefully pull the leather up, and wrap firmly around the sides. Press to adhere. At the corners, pinch the extra leather from each side together until it is smoothly adhered along the sides.

6. At the corners, fold the extra leather down flat (form triangles pointed toward the tips of the corners), and adhere to the back with diluted craft glue. Weight, and allow to dry thoroughly.

7. Cut a hole in the center of the leather covering the picture frame opening. Make your opening in the leather about 1 inch (2.5 cm) smaller than the frame opening.

8. Place the frame face down, and miter cut the corners of the leather. Pull up on the leather and adjust to fit in the corners. Take your time and create sharp corners before applying the spray adhesive. Once you have your leather properly trimmed, spray the inside edges and adhere.

9. Start at one corner and nail in the upholstery tacks all the way around. Space them evenly.

Note: It may be necessary to have a new piece of glass cut to fit, if you use very thick leather.

Cardboard Box Frame

Designed by Brandy Morgan

This clever box is made from foam core and cardboard. It's a nifty way to display a favorite snapshot, and you can store your other photos inside.

Tools

- *Pencil*
- *Ruler*
- *Utility knife*
- *Craft glue*
- *T-pins (optional)*
- *Artist's tape*

Materials

- *1 sheet foam core ⅛ inch (3 mm) thick*
- *Several sheets of colored corrugated cardboard*
- *Ribbon, optional*

Instructions

1. Measure and cut the following pieces of foam core:

* 2 pieces 6 x 8 inches (15 x 20 cm)

* 2 pieces 1¾ x 8 inches (4.5 x 20 cm)

* 2 pieces 1¾ x 5¾ inches (4.5 x 14.5 cm)

2. Select one of the 6 x 8-inch (15 x 20 cm) pieces of foam core and cut a piece of colored cardboard the same size. Glue the cardboard to the foam core. When the glue has set, place this piece on your work surface with the cardboard facing down. This will be the back of your box frame.

3. Select one of the 1¾- x 8-inch (4.5 x 20 cm) pieces of foam core, and cut a piece of colored cardboard 2 x 8 inches (5 x 20 cm). Glue the cardboard to the foam core, leaving ⅛ inch (3 mm) extended on the long sides. Allow to dry.

4. Repeat step 3 with the other 1¾- x 8-inch (4.5 x 20 cm) piece of foam core.

5. To create the long sides of the frame box, glue the pieces you made in steps 3 and 4 to the frame back. The extensions will cover the foam core edges. (Use T-pins to hold in place while glue sets, if necessary.)

6. Select one of the 1¾- x 5¾-inch (4.5 x 14.5 cm) pieces of foam core, and cut a piece of colored cardboard 2 x 6 inches (5 x 15 cm). Glue the cardboard to the foam core, leaving ⅛ inch (3 mm) extended on all sides. Allow to dry.

7. Repeat step 6 with the other 1¾- x 5¾-inch (4.5 x 14.5 cm) piece of foam core.

8. To create the short sides of the frame box, glue the pieces you made in steps 6 and 7 to the frame back. The extensions will cover the foam core edges. (Use T-pins to hold in place while glue sets, if necessary.)

9. Cut a 3 x 4-inch (7.5 x 10 cm) window in the remaining piece of foam core. (You may cut this window to whatever size you need, depending on your photo.)

10. Cut a piece of colored cardboard 6 x 8¼ inches (15 x 20.7 cm). Cut a window in the cardboard to match the one you cut in the foam core in step 9.

11. Glue the cardboard to the foam core, leaving a ⅛-inch (3 mm) extension on the two short sides. Allow to dry.

12. Mount your photo on the back of the frame face with artist's tape.

13. Cut two pieces of artist's tape about 3 inches (7.5 cm) each, and use as hinges on the inside of the box to secure the top.

14. Optional: To make a little handle, glue a loop of ribbon to the inside of the box top.

15. Decorate with cutouts of coordinated colored cardboard. (Say that three times real fast!)

Wild Wild West Frame

Designed by Brandy Morgan

This western-themed frame features a bandana-covered mat, a rodeo rope hanger, a bit of leather, and howlin' coyotes. Giddyap.

Tools
- *Ruler*
- *Pencil*
- *Drill (bit size corresponds to rope diameter)*
- *PVA craft glue*
- *Iron*
- *Scissors*
- *Spray adhesive*
- *Paintbrush*

Materials
- *8 x 10-inch (20 x 25 cm) wooden frame*
- *Heavy twine, rope, sisal, etc., 30 inches (75 cm) is used here*
- *Western-style decorative hardware—6 pieces**
- *2 strips of scrap leather ¼ x 8 inches (6 mm x 20 cm) each*
- *1 red bandana*
- *Mat board or cardboard*

*Hardware Note: Four rosettes with holes to accommodate the leather strips are used here. These are sold as mirror embellishments, and are available at your local hardware store. The two coyotes are charms from a bead shop with the rings snipped off. Stirrups, horseshoes, cowboy hats, cactus, etc., would all work equally well.

Instructions

1. Measure and lightly mark a line down the center of each side of your frame.

2. Measure and mark the holes for the hanging rope. Make them about ¼ the length of the frame from the top.

3. Drill the holes, and thread the rope through from the back. Tie knots in the ends that are at the front of the frame.

4. Fold one of the strips of leather in half and insert the folded end into the rosette hole from the front. Repeat with the other strip of leather and rosette.

5. Mark the positions of your western hardware pieces. Make sure they are evenly spaced. Apply a dab of glue at each position.

6. Press hardware pieces into the glue to adhere.

To make the bandana mat

7. Iron your bandana to remove any folds or wrinkles.

8. Lay the bandana facedown on your work surface.

9. Cut your mat board or cardboard to size, and spray it (the face) with the aerosol adhesive. (Read and follow manufacturer's instructions.)

10. Press mat (adhesive side down) onto the bandana. Apply even pressure to set the bond.

11. Cut the bandana flush with the outside edges of the mat. (The frame will hide this area.)

12. Cut a hole in the center of the bandana that's covering the mat window. Cut away the material, leaving just ¾ inch (1.9 cm) on all sides. Miter cut the fabric at each corner to within ⅛ inch (3 mm) of the mat.

13. Fold the material over the mat and adhere with diluted craft glue. Allow to dry.

14. Reassemble the frame with a picture of your favorite cowpoke.

Window of Opportunity Frame

Designed by Travis Waldron

Old windows make perfect picture frames. Whether you use a single or multi-pane, the creative opportunities are endless. The six panes here alternate earth-toned mat board with matted fiber art.

Tools
- *Paint scraper*
- *Wood putty*
- *Wire brush*
- *Sandpaper*
- *Compressed air*
- *Glazier points*
- *Point pusher*

Materials
- *Old window*
- *Glass (to fit)*
- *Mat board*
- *Artwork*
- *Foam core*

Instructions

1. The first step is to find a great old window. The older the better, but make sure it's structurally sound. Don't use a window that has any serious decay.

2. The next step is to clean up the window. Remove all the old glass and glazing material with a paint scraper. If some of the panes appear weak, fill in the joints with wood putty on the backside. How thorough you clean the window is a matter of personal taste, but the point is to clean it *minimally*. Use a wire brush, cloth, a bit of sandpaper—whatever you need to get rid of the dirt, but not the character. (Peeled and cracked paint has a way of sticking to wood. Use a can of compressed air or a ball of tape to remove all dust and residue from the rabbet area.)

3. Once you have the window cleaned, prepare the frame package. Clean your glass on both sides before putting it in place.

4. Put the mat, art, and backing into position quickly. A stray paint chip caught beneath the glass will drive you crazy.

5. Insert the glazier points with the point pusher to secure the package in place.

Use heavyweight hardware if you decide to hang the window. Window frames are very attractive when simply leaned against a wall. Consider making a pair of windows and adding antique hinges to create a fireplace or room screen. Remember, when you're searching for the "perfect" window to use, the rabbet must be able to accommodate at least a minimal frame package: glass, mat or spacer, art, and backing.

Creature Feature Frame

Designed by Travis Waldron

This delightful frame features little polymer clay creatures and a bright primary color scheme. It's as easy as child's play to make.

Tools
- *Paintbrush*
- *Masking tape*
- *Clear acrylic spray*
- *Baking sheet*
- *PVA craft glue*

Materials
- *8 x 10-inch (20 x 25 cm) frame*
- *Acrylic paints (white, green, yellow, red, and blue)*
- *Polymer sculpting clay (6 to 7 colors)*

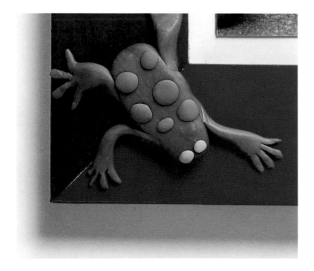

Instructions

1. Clean the surface of your frame, and prime it by painting it white. Use several coats if necessary. Allow to dry thoroughly.

2. Paint the frame as shown. Use the masking tape along the mitered corners to help you paint sharp edges. Make sure to paint the inside edges of your frame. Use at least two coats of paint for good coverage. Allow to dry.

3. Spray the frame with clear acrylic (read and follow manufacturer's instructions). Use several coats for a shiny finish.

4. Make creatures with sculpting clay, and bake according to manufacturer's instructions.

5. When creatures are cool (in terms of temperature), apply small dabs of glue to the backs of them and position them on the frame.

6. Let glue set and reassemble frame.

Lovely-in-Lace Frame

Designed by Brandy Morgan

What a lovely way to honor your ancestors. This old-fashioned frame is dressed up with dried flowers and lace, and trimmed with pretty-in-pink satin ribbon.

Tools
- *Paintbrushes*
- *Ruler*
- *Triangle*
- *Scissors*
- *PVA craft glue*

Materials
- *6 x 8-inch (15 x 20 cm) frame*
- *Acrylic paint—light green*
- *1 yard (9 m) lace (Width is determined by frame size. 2½-inch [6.25 cm] width is used here.)*
- *1 yard (.9 m) pink ribbon*
- *Dried flowers*

Instructions

1. Paint the frame with light green acrylic paint. Allow to dry. Apply a second coat if needed.

2. Cut two 8-inch (20 cm) pieces of lace and two 6-inch (15 cm) pieces. Miter cut the ends to fit the face of your frame.

3. Dilute PVA glue with water, and brush the solution onto the face of the frame.

4. Position lace pieces so that the inside edges are flush with the frame window and the outside edges overlap the frame by about ¼ inch (6 mm). Line up the mitered ends carefully so you have a neat fit.

5. Brush glue mixture onto the sides of the frame. Fold the lace over the sides, and press to adhere.

6. Cut the ribbon to the size of the window. Miter cut the ends.

7. Apply glue to the window edge, and press the strips of ribbon into place.

8. Make two bouquets of dried flowers—one big and one small. Tie the flowers with ribbon at the base.

9. Apply full-strength glue to the backs of the ribbon, and adhere to frame. Allow to dry.

Tic-Tac-Toe

Designed by Travis Waldron

Here's a hinged set of frames with a fun-and-games finish. This simple project is twice as nice for pictures of twins or perfectly sweet as a Valentine's Day gift.

Tools
- *Paintbrush*
- *Straightedge and pencil*
- *Hand saw*
- *Coarse sandpaper*
- *Drill with small bit*
- *Screwdriver*

Materials
- *Two 5 x 7-inch (12.5 x 17.5 cm) picture frames*
- *Acrylic paint-gray, white, and red*
- *Two small hinges*

Instructions

1. Paint both frames with gray acrylic paint. (Be sure to paint all of the frame surfaces, since all are visible with a tabletop display.) Allow to dry.

2. Paint one frame red and one frame white. Allow to dry.

3. Using a straightedge and pencil, extend the lines of the picture frame opening to create the tic-tac-toe lines.

4. Carefully saw into the lines you've marked to a depth of about $1/16$ inch (1.5 mm).

5. Paint Xs and Os as shown. Use white on the red frame and red on the white frame. Allow to dry thoroughly.

6. Roughly sand until the desired level of "distress" is achieved. (You may omit this step if you already have enough distress in your life.)

7. Mark the positions of the hinge holes. Use a drill bit smaller than the hinge screws, and make starter holes. Screw in the hinges.

8. Assemble the frames using your favorite photos.

Note: You may draw or paint the tic-tac-toe lines if you prefer not to saw.

Log Cabin Frame

Designed by Travis Waldron

You may not have a cabin in the woods, but you can add a rustic feel to any room with this cozy frame. Sticks, glue, and bathtub caulk are your basic building materials.

Tools
- *Paintbrush*
- *Pruning shears*
- *Glue gun and glue sticks*
- *Rag and water*
- *¾-inch (1.9 cm) wood chisel and hammer (Optional)*

Materials
- *8 x 10-inch (20 x 25 cm) frame (with flat profile)*
- *White acrylic paint*
- *Straight twigs*
- *Tube of white acrylic caulk (tub and tile)*

Instructions
1. Paint your frame white, and allow to dry.

2. Select the straightest twigs you can find. Snip off any small branches or knots.

3. For the large "logs," cut eight twigs 10 inches (25 cm) long. For the smaller side "logs," cut 18 pieces 2 inches (5 cm) long. (Note: Measurements will vary depending on what size frame you're using and how big your twigs are.)

4. Heat your glue gun. Apply a line of glue near the top edge of the frame. Position the first log on the glue. Leave a small space, and apply another line of glue. Position your second log. Repeat this process until you reach the bottom of your frame.

5. Now you're ready to apply the caulking, or "chinking." Have a small dish of water and a rag handy before you begin. (This can get a bit messy.)

6. Beginning at the top of the frame, apply a thin bead of caulk between the logs. Wet your fingertip and use it to smooth the caulk. Make sure you use enough caulk to fill in nicely. Use your rag to keep your hands and the frame tidy. Allow to dry.

7. Optional: Split a 10-inch (25 cm) twig using a ¾-inch (1.9 cm) wood chisel and hammer. Use these split logs to cover the top and bottom edges of the frame. Adhere with the glue gun and caulk.

8. Optional: To add more depth to the sides, cut a twig into ¼-inch (6 mm) slices. Adhere the slices to the sides using the glue gun.

Hunt Club

Designed by Travis Waldron

This old carved frame was found in a junk shop. It had a dozen coats of paint on it, but absolutely no character. Just look what a little stain and gold wax can do. This old carved clunker is now a classic—fit for the fox and hounds.

Tools
- *Paintbrush*
- *180 to 200 grit sandpaper*
- *Tack cloth*
- *Soft cloth*

Materials
- *20 x 24-inch (50 x 60 cm) frame*
- *Mahogany wood stain*
- *Wax metallic finish (gold)*
- *Mineral spirits*

Instructions

1. Remove the glass and mounting materials from picture frame. Clean as needed.

2. Apply a thin coat of stain to the entire frame, and allow to dry overnight. Thoroughly clean your brush with the mineral spirits.

3. Lightly sand the frame and wipe clean with the tack cloth.

4. Apply a second coat of stain, and allow to dry overnight. Clean your brush. (Repeat this step if you want a heavier/darker finish.)

5. Place the thoroughly dried frame face up on a flat work surface. (Read and follow the instructions for the particular metallic wax product you choose.)

6. Apply a small amount of the wax with your finger (or cotton swab) to the raised surface of the frame. (You might also want to apply a thin coat to the lip of the frame to highlight.)

7. Polish with a soft cloth for a rich sheen.

Notebook Frame

Designed by Travis Waldron

Here's a clever and crafty way to display your favorite little scholar's picture. Paint and colored pencils create the ruled paper look. Copper wire and a few drilled holes make the spiral binding. It's as easy as ABC.

Tools

- *Pencil*
- *Ruler*
- *Drill and ³/₃₂-inch (2.5 cm) bit*
- *Sandpaper*
- *Paintbrush*
- *Spray acrylic*
- *Needle-nose pliers (with wire cutter)*

Materials

- *5 x 7-inch (12.5 x 17.5 cm) frame*
- *Scrap piece of wood*
- *White acrylic paint*
- *Light blue and red colored pencils*
- *18-gauge copper wire*
  - * about 14 inches (35 cm) long*

Instructions

1. Remove all the glass and mounting materials from picture frame. Place a scrap piece of wood on your work surface to protect it. Put the frame on your work surface faceup in the portrait position.

2. Measure and mark a vertical line ¼ inch (6 mm) from the left edge of the frame.

3. Measure and mark wire holes every ½ inch (1.3 cm) along this line.

4. Drill the holes.

5. Sand the frame until it's smooth.

6. Apply a liberal coat of white paint to the entire frame, and allow it to dry. Do not allow paint to clog drilled holes. Repeat with a second coat for thorough coverage, if needed.

7. About 1 inch (2.5 cm) from the top of the frame, draw a horizontal line with the light blue colored pencil. Repeat, spacing lines every ³/₈ inch (9 mm).

8. Draw a vertical line with the red colored pencil ³/₄ inch (1.9 cm) from the left edge of the frame. Draw a second one, right next to it.

9. Spray the frame with clear acrylic finish and allow it to dry.

10. Insert the wire from the back of the frame through the top hole, until you have ½ inch (1.3 cm) left in the back. Hold this tail against the frame to anchor it.

11. Wrap the wire in spiral fashion through the remaining holes. End at the back side, and trim to a ½-inch (1.3 cm) tail.

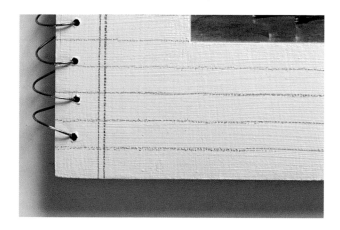

Silver Button Frame

Designed by Travis Waldron

This stylish frame features matte silver paint and flat carved buttons. The carved pattern is repeated on the sides with a woodburner.

Tools

- *Sharp pencil*
- *Drill with a $1/16$-inch (1.5 mm) bit*
- *Sandpaper and toothpicks (if needed)*
- *Wood burning tool*

Materials

- *6 x 8-inch (15 x 20 cm) frame*
- *8 flat buttons with design—1 inch (2.5 cm) buttons are used*
- *Silver acrylic paint*
- *1 yard (.9 m) of color-coordinated waxed linen*

Instructions

1. Measure and mark the position of the buttons. (This will vary depending on the size of your frame and the dimension of your buttons.) Measure the width of one side of the frame, and divide that number in half. This is the middle. Lightly draw a line from end to end at this middle point.

2. Lay out the buttons along this line, and space them evenly. Use your sharp pencil to mark the position of the buttonholes.

3. Drill holes at the marks you've made.

4. If you want a primitive, more natural look to your frame, sand it before you paint. Sanding against the wood grain will provide a rough and ready surface.

5. Paint the entire frame with the silver paint. (Again, if your intent is to create a natural look, don't worry about brush strokes.) Make sure you keep the drill holes paint-free. Use toothpicks, if necessary. Allow to dry.

6. To attach the buttons, thread a 5-inch (12.5 cm) piece of waxed linen through the buttonhole, then through the corresponding holes on the frame. Securely tie at the back of the frame. Repeat for all the buttons.

7. Heat the woodburning tool.

8. Measure and mark the center points of the two remaining sides. Lightly draw the button design at these points. (Don't worry about copying it exactly. It's just the suggestion of the pattern.)

9. Use the woodburner to trace over the design. Be careful not to burn too deep.

Fabric-Covered Mirror Frame

Designed by Tammy Lou Grant

With some bold fabric and a bit of quilter's batting, this drab mirror became downright dazzling. No sewing required.

Tools
- *Pencil or fabric marker*
- *Scissors*
- *Craft glue*
- *Old paintbrush*
- *Spray adhesive*

Materials
- *Oval frame and mirror to fit*
- *1 yard (.9 m) fabric (Any sturdy cotton will work fine. (Avoid lightweight and sheer materials.)*
- *Polyester quilter's batting*

Instructions

1. Lay your fabric face down on a clean work surface. Place your frame on the fabric and trace around the edges of the frame with your pencil or fabric marker.

2. Now, add about 2 inches (5 cm) to the outside edge line and 2 inches (5 cm) to the inside edge line. (This extra is needed so you can wrap your material around the frame, after the batting has been added. If you're using a particularly deep frame, or if you want an extra puffy look, you might want to add a little extra batting.) Cut the fabric and set it aside.

3. Cut your batting into strips to fit the face of your frame. Cut enough strips to evenly cover the frame at least twice. Add extra layers for extra puff. (Remember that the material has to wrap around the batting.)

4. Mix a solution of half glue and half water. Cover the surface of the frame with the glue mixture using an old paintbrush.

5. Place the batting strips on the frame and lightly press to make a bond. Continue until you have covered the surface of your frame.

6. Brush another coat of glue mixture on the first layer of batting. Place the second layer of batting strips on top of the first, and press to adhere. (Continue in this manner for extra layers.)

7. Place fabric face down on work surface. Spray top layer of batting with adhesive, and position on fabric. Press lightly to assist bond. (Read and follow spray adhesive manufacturer's instructions.)

8. When the bond has set, turn the frame over.

9. In order to wrap your material around the oval frame smoothly, you'll need to cut a series of notches into the edges. (figure 18). The depth of your notches will depend on the bulk of your batting and size of your frame.

10. Apply the diluted glue to the back of the frame along the outer edge. Fold the fabric over and adhere. Repeat this process with the inner edge. Cut off excess.

11. The notches along the inside edge will be reflected once you install the mirror, so you need to cover them up. Place the mirror in the frame and see just how much space needs to be covered. (Your particular style of frame will determine how wide you need to cut your cover strips.)

12. Cut cover strips of fabric, and glue them around the inside edge of the frame to hide the reflection of the notches.

13. Allow to dry. Install your mirror and hang.

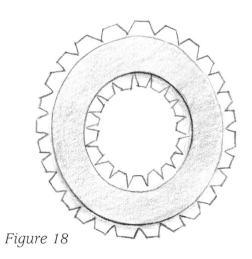

Figure 18

String-Wrapped Frame

Designed by Tammy Lou Grant

Here's a great rainy day project for you and the kids to get all wrapped up in.
You'll need string, cardboard, and just a few tools.

Tools

- *Scissors*
- *PVA craft glue*

Materials

- *5 x 7-inch (12.5 x 17.5 cm) frame form of heavy cardboard or balsa wood*
- *5 spools of colorful twine (neon nylon is used here, but you could also use dyed hemp, embroidery floss, or yarn)*
- *Scrap cardboard or foam core, approximately 8 x 10 inches (20 x 25 cm)*

This little frame is most attractive when care is used in the wrapping process. Each wrap of twine should be snug against the next. If you're making this with the kids, you'll want to demonstrate the proper wrapping technique for them. To finish the corners, the string is coiled into squares.

Instructions

1. Cut a length of string that's comfortable to work with.

2. To start the wrap, apply a small dab of glue to the back of your frame. Press the end of your first length of string into the glue, and hold it in place while you begin to wrap.

3. Continue wrapping until you near the end of the first piece of string. Tie the second length of string (the second color) to the end of the first. Make sure the knot is at the back of the frame. Continue wrapping.

4. When you get near the corner of the frame, turn the frame 90° and continue wrapping on the next side. You will leave the corner unwrapped.

5. When you've wrapped the entire frame (except the corners), glue the tail end of the string to the back.

6. To create the corner coils, select your string color and glue one end to the back of the frame. Hold it in place, until it has adhered.

7. Spread the exposed corner with a thin layer of glue.

8. Coil the string into the shape of a square. Make sure the string lies even and snug.

9. When you reach the end of the coil (the center of the square), cut your string and press it down to ensure a good bond. If you need to add a bit more glue to the end, do so. Allow to dry.

10. To cover the exposed corner edges, coat with a thin layer of glue. Cut string to fit and hold in place until secured.

To create the back of the frame

11. Cut four 1-inch (2.5 cm) squares of cardboard.

12. Glue the cardboard squares into corners.

13. Cut a piece of cardboard or foam core slightly smaller than the frame.

14. Spread a thin layer of glue on each of the corner cardboard squares, and press the back into place. Weight it down and allow to dry.

To create a back stand

15. Cut a piece of cardboard 1 x 3 inches (2.5 x 7.5 cm). Measure down about 1 inch (2.5 cm) and make a slight fold.

16. Glue the portion above the fold to the back of the frame, and allow to dry.

17. Insert the picture. (This frame will accommodate wallet-size or school pictures.)

Dragonfly Clip Frames

Designed by Travis Waldron

One design plus two techniques equals a bunch of fun. Use the dragonfly template on page 109, and then decide to paint or etch. Why not try both?

This design is for an 8 x 10-inch (20 x 25 cm) clip frame with space for a 4 x 6-inch (10 x 15 cm) picture.

Etched Dragonflies

Tools

- *Craft knife*
- *Craft stick*
- *Paintbrush (number 6)*
- *Glass cleaner*
- *Paper towel*

Materials

- *8 x 10-inch (20 x 25 cm) clip frame*
- *Clear adhesive-backed shelf paper*
- *Etching solution*

Instructions

1. Thoroughly clean the glass.

2. Place the template face up on a clean work surface.

3. Place the glass on top the of template.

4. Cut a piece of transparent shelf paper to fit the frame. Peel off the backing and adhere to the glass. (You will be able to see the template beneath.)

5. Using your craft knife, trace the design (cut it) onto the shelf paper. Lift off the paper as you work to expose the glass. Work slowly and carefully. The areas that become exposed will be the areas that are etched.

6. Use the craft stick to gently burnish all the edges. This will ensure crisp edges and prevent the etching solution from leaking under the paper.

7. Apply the etching solution. (Read and follow manufacturer's instructions.)

8. Clean the solution off the glass (according to the package directions), and towel dry. Remove the shelf paper, and clean the glass with glass cleaner.

Painted Dragonflies

Tools

- *Isopropyl alcohol*
- *Paintbrushes (numbers 6 and 2)*
- *Glass cleaner*
- *Paper towels*

Materials

- *8 x 10-inch (20 x 25 cm) clip frame*
- *Glass paints (heat-set paints in red, orange, yellow, gold, green, and black)*

Instructions

1. Thoroughly clean the glass, then wipe it down with alcohol. (Handle the glass only by the edges to ensure that it remains clean and oil-free.)

2. Place the template face up on a clean work surface, and position the glass on top.

3. Use brush number 6 to paint the dragonflies and grass stalks. Allow to dry.

4. Use brush number 2 to paint black accents on the dragonfly bodies and wings. Apply small dots or thin lines. Allow to dry 24 hours.

5. Bake the glass according to paint manufacturer's instructions. Let the glass cool completely, and clean with glass cleaner.

6. Re-assemble the clip frame with mat board or construction paper between the glass and backing. Don't forget your favorite picture.

Copper Vase Frame

Designed by Travis Waldron

Here's a little frame with a lot of class. It's trimmed with embossed, oxidized copper and a miniature vase. Add a dried or fresh flower, a feather, or beads.

Tools

- *Drill with small bit*
- *Paintbrush*
- *Tin snips, old scissors, or garden shears*
- *180-grit sandpaper or emery board*
- *Candle*
- *Needle-nose pliers, or tweezers*
- *Rag or paper towel*
- *Pencil*
- *Awl or nail*
- *Small hammer*

Materials

- *5 x 7-inch (12.5 x 17.5 cm) picture frame*
- *1 florist stem tube (glass or plastic)*
- *Dark green acrylic paint*
- *36-gauge copper sheeting*
  * *2 pieces cut 1 x 3 inches (2.5 x 7.5 cm) each*
- *Small copper brads*
- *Copper foil ¼ inch (6 mm) wide (optional)*
  * *1 piece cut 2 inches (5 cm)*
- *20-gauge copper wire*
  * *2 pieces cut 8 inches (20 cm) each*

Instructions

1. Determine the position of the florist tube. Mark two points (one near the top and one near the bottom) on each side of the tube. This is where the wire will go to hold the tube in place. Drill holes through the frame at each mark.

2. Paint the entire frame. Be careful to keep the holes you drilled paint-free. Dry completely.

3. After you've cut the two strips of copper sheeting using your tin snips or scissors, lightly sand the edges until smooth.

4. Light your candle. Hold a copper strip by one of its corners with the tweezers or pliers. Position the strip over the candle flame until it oxidizes. Do not overheat.

5. Cool the strip completely. Wipe off the soot with a rag or paper towel.

6. Repeat steps 4 and 5 with the second copper strip.

7. Lay the copper strips on a clean work surface with the oxidized side down. Using a pencil (with a dull rounded tip) draw a design on one of the strips. Apply enough pressure to indent, so the design will appear on the oxidized side. Repeat with the second strip.

8. Position each strip on the frame-oxidized side up. Use your awl (or hammer and nail) and make holes for the copper brads. To secure the strips into the frame, lightly tap the brads in.

9. Optional: Wrap about 2 inches (5 cm) of copper foil around the edge of the florist's tube. Leave ⅛ inch (3 mm) extended beyond the top. Fold the extended portion over the lip, to the inside of the tube. Alternatively, you could use copper colored paint to create a copper edge.

10. Thread one piece of copper wire through the upper right hole you drilled in step 1. Leave about 2 inches (5 cm) on the back side of the frame. Loop the wire around the florist's tube and through the upper left hole. Make a second loop around the tube. At the back of the frame, twist the ends together to secure and trim.

11. Repeat step 10 with the second piece of wire to make the lower loop.

Wire-Wrapped Frames

Designed by Linda Rose Nall

Add a hot new look to old metal frames with wire wrapping. Mix in your favorite beads, blobs, and charms, and you've got something special all wrapped up.

Tools
- *Wire cutters*
- *Needle-nose pliers*
- *Glue gun and glue sticks (or silicone tube glue)*

Materials
- *Two 5 x 7-inch (12.5 x 17.5 cm) silver frames*
- *20-gauge wire (silver, copper, or gold)*
- *Assorted beads and glass blobs (jewels)*
- *Charms, trinkets, buttons, etc. (optional)*

Metal frames can be wonderfully embellished with wire and baubles. The key is to create a stable wire structure by securely anchoring the wire or wires to at least one corner of the frame. Make sure that the wire does not interfere with the rabbet area of the frame, or impede proper picture insertion.

Instructions

1. Begin the wire wrap at the back of the upper left corner. Hold one end securely at the back of the frame, and wrap it around the corner once. Twist the short "tail" end around the other wire until tight. Press snugly against the back of the frame. (This will anchor the wire.)

2. Bring the wire across the (top) back of the frame, and wrap it around the front of the right corner from the lower right to upper left. Bring it around to the back of the frame.

3. Loop the wire around the piece of wire you've been holding secure, creating a loose simple knot. Press against the back. This is the basic wire foundation.

4. Continue to curve and curl this wire (using the needle-nose pliers), ending with a spiral. Attach each new wire you wish to use by twisting it onto the wire that runs across the back of the frame. Then bring it to the front, and shape as desired.

5. Add the beads of your choice (coordinate with the colors of your photo or artwork) to create fun and whimsical designs.

6. Heat the glue gun (or use silicone tube glue).

7. Glass blobs are added to help secure the wire to the frame. Apply a small amount of glue on the wire, and press a blob into it. Hold in place until it's secure. Allow to dry overnight.

8. Repeat for the second frame.

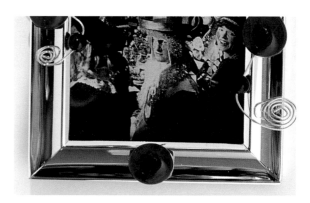

Heavy Metal Frame

Designed by Travis Waldron

Here's a high-tech look. This sleek, modern frame is made with metal braces, mending plates, and machine screws. Assembling the hardware for this frame just might take you back to the days of erector sets.

Tools
- *Pliers*

Materials
- *8 x 10-inch (20 x 25 cm) glass or acrylic*
- *8 x 10-inch (20 x 25 cm) mat board with window*
- *8 x 10-inch (20 x 25 cm) backing board*
- *8 corner braces 3-1/2 x 5/8 inch (8.8 x 1.6 cm)*
- *20 machine screws, 3/4 inch (#8-32) (1.9 cm)*
- *20 nuts (#8-32)*
- *2 mending plates 3 x 5/8 inches (7.5 x 1.6 cm)*
- *6 mending plates 4 x 5/8 inches (10 x 1.6 cm)*
- *Black jack chain, 1 foot (30 cm) in length*

During the assembly of this project *do not* over-tighten the screws. Overtightening will make assembly difficult and could cause the glazing to crack. Make your final tightening adjustments *after* the frame is fully assembled.

Instructions
1. Assemble the glass, mat, photo or art, and backing. Place this frame package face up on a clean work surface.

2. Place two corner braces at each corner. Put one brace on top of the glass and one under the backing.

3. Line up the holes in the braces, and insert screws into the two holes closest to the corner tips. Add nuts to the screws from the back side of the frame. Leave the nuts loose—providing some support, but not tightened.

4. Place one 3-inch (7.5 cm) mending plate between the two corner braces on the glass at the top edge of the frame. Line up the holes with the corner braces, and attach with screws and nuts. This creates the frame top. (Note: There is no back mending plate used here.)

5. Repeat step 4 to create the frame bottom.

6. To create the left side of the frame: Place one 4-inch (10 cm) mending plate along the left edge of the glass. Line up the top hole in the mending plate with the bottom hole of the corner brace, and attach with screw and nut.

7. Place another 4-inch (10 cm) mending plate along the left edge of the glass. Line up the bottom hole in the mending plate with the top hole of the corner brace, and attach with screw. (Note: The two mending plates on the left side will overlap.)

8. To complete the left side: Place a 4-inch (10 cm) mending plate on the bottom, against the backing. Line up the holes on the mending plates, and attach with screws and nuts. (Note: The last hole on the bottom mending plate is lined up and attached to the bottom corner brace.)

9. Repeat steps 6, 7, and 8 to create the right side of the frame.

10. To attach the chain to the frame, use either the two inside or outside screws on the top edge. Remove the appropriate nuts at the back of the frame. Move the screws up, and insert the chain. Lower the screws back through the chain link, and replace the nuts.

11. Tighten all nuts to make certain that the frame is secure. Be extremely cautious not to use too much pressure.

Indian Quill Frame

Designed by Travis Waldron

Native Americans used porcupine quills to embellish all sorts of accessories. This simple frame is dyed to give it a rustic feel and features the traditional chevron symbol.

Tools
- *Sandpaper (100 grit)*
- *Isopropyl alcohol*
- *Measuring cup and measuring spoons*
- *Old glass jar with tight-fitting lid*
- *Paintbrushes*
- *Clear acrylic spray*
- *Scissors*
- *PVA craft glue*

Materials
- *5 x 7-inch (12.5 x 17.5 cm) frame*
- *Burgundy fabric dye (powdered)*
- *Porcupine quills (Porcupine quills are available in better bead and jewelry-supply shops.)*

Instructions

1. Sand the frame to rough up the surface.

2. Mix approximately 1 tablespoon (15 mL) of fabric dye with 1 cup (.24 L) of alcohol in the glass jar. Shake until dissolved. (If using liquid dye, use ½ cup [.12 L] of alcohol.) Alcohol is used instead of water to mix the dye, since water causes the grain of the wood to rise and takes longer to dry.

3. Paint the frame with the dye. Allow to dry. Repeat until desired color is achieved.

4. After the frame is completely dry, spray with clear acrylic to seal. Dry and repeat.

5. Select quills of similar length and diameter. Use scissors to blunt cut the root end of the quill. (The root end has a small pin-like extension.)

6. Practice your design by arranging quills in chevron pattern at one mitered corner of the frame. This will allow you to determine the glue area and the number of quills needed.

7. Mix a solution of half glue and half water. Apply the solution to the frame with a paintbrush in small sections. Arrange the quills and press them into the glue to adhere.

8. Continue until design is complete. Repeat on opposite corner.

9. On the remaining corners apply glue and three long quills, as shown. Allow to dry.

10. Optional: When the glue is completely dry, you may spray with several more coats of the clear acrylic sealer.

hanging it up

Arranging and Hanging Pictures

It all started out so innocently...you thought you'd try a new craft, expand your creative expression, and recycle a few of those old frames from up in the attic. But the prospect of actually *hanging* your pictures has you filled with dread. It's true, there is something about arranging and hanging pictures that can stop even the most confident home decorator dead in her tracks. And that's a shame because arranging and rearranging what's on your walls is one of the easiest and least expensive things you can do to give an old room a new look. (The truth is, most of us stop noticing pictures that never change position, so if you're not in a state of domestic bliss, maybe it's time you rearranged your pictures.) If all that clean white wall space has you feeling intimidated read on a bit and you'll discover that displaying your pictures can be a real pleasure.

Style

Your unique taste and manner are reflected in the way you decorate, design, and inhabit your home. Some of us prefer a *less is more*, minimalist, uncluttered look, while others favor abundant furnishings and a more copious decor. Some of us prefer conservative and traditional decorating schemes, while others like a more unconventional, unpredictable look. Some of us have deep pockets when it comes to decorating our homes, while others take a more frugal, even thrifty approach. We have certain size rooms to work with, distinct styles of furniture, particular types of floor coverings and window treatments, and unique collections of bric-a-brac. No matter what your personal style happens to be, when it comes to hanging and arranging pictures, there's plenty of sound advice that you can adapt to suit your personal preferences.

Height

Contemporary decorating is more casual and practical than traditional interior design.

Traditional design is more formal and symmetrical in appearance. Traditionally, pictures were displayed in large groups hung high on a wall. Today the trend is to allow more wall space to surround artwork and to hang it lower, for more casual, seated viewing. Pictures hung too high are visually out of reach, they tend to dominate rather than invite, and they appear disconnected from everything else in the room. So, unless your intent is to draw the viewer's attention upward (perhaps to admire a beautiful moulding or ceiling treatment), it's better to go a few inches too low, rather than too high. Since hanging pictures too high is still one of the most common home decorating errors, here's an easy rule of thumb to follow—position the *center* of your artwork about 5 (1.5 cm) feet off the floor. In some instances, it makes sense to hang pictures a bit higher than you ordinarily would. Large-scale works can often be hung higher to good advantage. Hallways really do present great decorating opportunities. Not only is eye-level higher, but you don't have to worry about relating to furniture. You can hang high (and low), and use pictures and artwork almost as wall covering. Hallways are particularly good locations for small detailed pictures, where the viewer can enjoy a more intimate viewing experience. (Keep in mind that large expansive pictures—broad landscapes, for instance—will tend to look confined and claustrophobic in a hallway setting.)

Off the Wall

There are many ways to display your pictures without turning your walls into Swiss cheese. So, if you're timid about the hammer and nail thing, or if you've already run out of wall space, consider going off the wall. Ledges, easels, shelves, mantels, and tabletops are all visually intimate areas and picture perfect display opportunities. Displaying your pictures off the wall allows for greater enjoyment of small detailed works, easy replacement and removal, and spontaneous rearranging.

◀ A fine collection of Asian calligraphy. Notice that the largest, most dynamic print is quite high on the wall. This print is robust enough to warrant the height, without appearing top heavy or disconnected. (While we're on the subject of large pictures—big bold pieces are particularly well-paired with oversized furnishings.) In addition, in high traffic areas (where people walk or stand), such as hallways, landings, and foyers, "eye-level" is necessarily higher, so you can hang your pictures high with confidence in these locations.

▶ The piano-top collection of framed family photos has a distinctly intimate feel. This warm and inviting ambiance is created by casually layering or overlapping the pictures and by the eclectic mix of frame styles. Notice too how the pictures on the wall lead the eye to the collection.

▲ Dinner guests are treated to a wonderful meal and the aesthetic pleasure of a collection of fine prints propped on wainscoting moulding. The pictures also echo the color and shape of the paneled wainscoting.

◀ You can add an air of distinction to a special piece of artwork by displaying it on an easel. Easels are available in a variety of styles from ultramodern stainless steel to traditional carved wood. It is customary that the style of the easel reflects the style of the artwork and frame.

▼ If your refrigerator has become a magnet for displaying pictures and kids' art work, check this out. What do you get when you cross an empty CD case with a refrigerator magnet and your favorite photo? A great way to enjoy your picture, while keeping it safe from sticky fingerprints. There's even room for mat board inside this plastic "frame".

▶ A great way to show off your snapshots, or in this case, antique postcards—is in a bouquet display. Needle-nose pliers are used to curl the ends of paper-covered craft wire. The pictures are then inserted in the curls and arranged in a favorite vase.

Where oh Where?

Anyone can hang a group of pictures in that obvious space above a couch, but what about the not so obvious spaces? Use your creative energy to hang pictures in curious places. A bit of whimsy and surprise can create a most remarkable room. Look around *your* house...see all that space above doorways and windows, and don't forget all that unused area between your floor and your windowsills. (Of course, if you have pets or small children this space may be better left alone.) Closet doors, particularly those used infrequently, are wonderful places to hang pictures. Most of us have all sorts of available wall space we're not using.

▲ Notice how these two prints wonderfully enhance the space. This is already a visually busy area and it would be just fine to leave the wall space empty. However, the addition of pictures transforms the ordinary into the extraordinary.

▼ See how nicely a trio of framed prints fills an awkward area on a stairway wall.

Integrating Pictures and Accessories

Besides using your wall space more creatively and getting your pictures off the wall all together, there's another way you can enhance your home with pictures. By paying attention to your existing decorative objects—being mindful of color, texture, shape, and style—you can integrate and cleverly combine your pictures and artwork with your accessories and collectibles, such as baskets, shells, trivets, and antiques of all sorts.

► This charming cottage bathroom is decorated with a combination of pictures, both leaning and hung, and accessories. The assortment of pictures would look odd without the antique mirror, Chinese basket, and candle collection.

◄ The eye is drawn to the dramatic vases on the floor at the bottom of the staircase. Notice how the clever placement of the picture on the floor takes advantage of our attention. The shape and color of the vases is repeated with the lamp and again a picture is positioned (to the right of the lamp) to capitalize on our attention. These pictures and decorative objects are well integrated and create a visually pleasing harmony, but without the vases, the picture placement wouldn't make sense.

▲ Here's a dynamic impression created by repeating color, shape, and texture. The tropical Florida theme is achieved by establishing a relationship between the pictures and tabletop accessories. Leaning the square picture in the center solidifies the relationship. When thinking of ways to combine your framed pictures with your home accessories, you can add interest and balance by mixing curved pieces with all the hard angular edges of the frames.

Alternatives to Wire

Using decorative cord, ribbon, or even chain, to suspend pictures is an eye-catching and inexpensive way to cover more wall space, without investing in more artwork. In addition, unusual hanging treatments can add interest and appeal to even your more mundane prints.

◄ ▲ Look at these lovely wireless treatments. Pretty botanical prints are hung from the crown moulding with decorative rope and ribbon in this lavender dressing room. This old-fashioned touch not only fills more wall space, but adds a bit of romance to this feminine sanctuary.

▲ A mirror framed in an antique mantel is suspended from the moulding with decorative rope and fancy rosettes. The richness of the wood, the warmth of the red accents, and the elegant glow of the candles temper the formal tone. (Decorative cord is often used just for show—the pictures are actually hung in the traditional manner using screw eyes, wire, and picture hangers, then the cord is attached. If you choose to hang your pictures using cord, make certain the weight of your picture is properly supported. Consult your local frame shop for advice.)

Avoiding Damage

Environmental hazards: Smoke, direct sunlight, heat, moisture, and condensation-can all wreak havoc on framed art. Think about where these potential dangers exist in your home.

If your artwork has monetary or sentimental value, hanging it over the fireplace mantel might be risky business. Depending on the type and condition of your fireplace, this traditional practice can increase the likelihood of damage by exposure to smoke and soot. Of course, if you don't use your fireplace, you're safe. If you do, you can always rearrange your pictures during the wood-burning season. While we're on the subject of smoke, long-term exposure to cigarette smoke can also be quite damaging to your fine paper and fiber art. One more reason to kick the habit.

Similarly, prolonged exposure to direct sunlight will fade your artwork and mat board. You may want to think twice about hanging a picture or framed needlework where it will be in the sun all day. UV-protected glass acts like a sunscreen but all-day direct exposure will take its toll in time. Speaking of light, the once-popular picture lights (those lights attached to the tops of frames) seem to have fallen from fashion, but you can now purchase cordless picture lights that run on batteries. If you don't have sufficient ambient light for enjoyable viewing of your pictures, consider installing concealed or track lights to emphasize them.

Frequent changes in humidity and a consistently high humidity are hazardous to paper art. Therefore, bathrooms (with frequently used tubs or showers) are not the place for hanging treasured pictures. Assuming someone in your house cooks, give careful consideration before hanging works of value or original works in your kitchen—the changes in temperature, smoke, and grease all pose threats to paper and textile art. If you use a humidifier or room mister for houseplants or personal comfort, do not place them in close proximity to your pictures. Indoor hot tubs, saunas, and solariums are all areas to stay away from. Likewise, keep your pictures a safe distance from steam radiators. Candles, oil lamps, and wall lanterns should all be used with caution and not used too near pictures.

Physical hazards: When deciding where to hang your pictures, be on the lookout for cabinet or chest doors that can swing open and knock a picture off the wall. Frequently used (i.e., *slammed*) sliding glass doors can create enough vibration in a wall to cause a picture to fall. Television antennas (*rabbit ears*) and billiard cue sticks have been the downfall of more than a few pictures.

Grouping and Placement

When grouping pictures, there are two broad styles: formal and informal. *Formal* is more traditional, symmetrical, structured, linear, and generally neater looking. *Informal* is more relaxed, flexible, inviting, and generally more creative looking.

Within these two broad styles are a host of arrangements that are simple to duplicate. There are no strict rules for grouping pictures, so feel free to experiment and do what you like! Here are a couple more tips:

- If a picture isn't large enough to look substantial over a couch or seating area, put a smaller piece (or pieces) on either side of it.

- An odd number of pictures grouped together is more interesting than an even number.

- Don't make your grouped pictures *wider* than the furniture over which they hang.

▶ A classic example of a formal grouping.

▶ An informal style.

Don't leave more than 1 foot (30 cm) of blank wall space between your furniture and your pictures.

Small, delicate pictures can easily get lost on a busy background. Dynamically painted or covered walls (patterned wallpaper, textured or rag-roll painted, or paper bag or burlap covered) deserve large bold pictures in substantial frames.

Regardless of the arrangement you choose, before you start making holes in your wall, you need to do the following floor exercises.

Determining Placement

First, drop the hammer. When you're trying to figure out how to group and position your pictures, it's best to actually start on your floor. Grab a friend, neighbor, or family member too—it really helps to have another pair of eyes.

1. Start by determining how much wall space you want to fill. Measure and mark your dimension on the wall.

2. Then, transfer your dimensions to the floor and mark with masking tape.

3. Next, lay your framed pictures out on the floor. Mix things up until you see a combination that pleases. (If you need a bit of direction here, try putting your largest piece in the lower left corner and work out from there. Or use one of the grouping illustrations for inspiration.)

4. Now make paper cutouts of each of your pieces.

5. Tape these to the wall to fine-tune your positioning. If you have a hard time with commitment, you might want to leave your cutouts up for 24 hours until you're sure you're happy with the arrangement.

6. When exhaustion finally gets the better of you, it's time to make some holes in your wall!

Here are some ideas for arrangements. Remember you can add a mirror, wreath, clock, plate, or other accents to the mix for added interest and appeal.

Stair Stepping

The stairway wall can be quite a creative challenge. Step your pictures to follow the line of your stairs (figure 19). Notice that the center points of the pictures are aligned diagonally. This diagonal placement style works well in a stairway, but is visually disconcerting in most other areas.

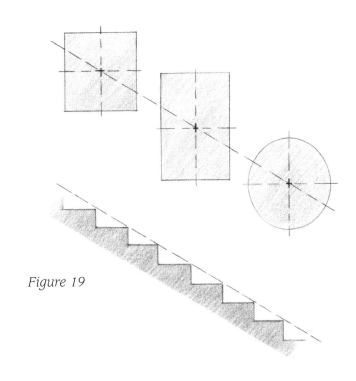

Figure 19

Figure 20

Tops in Alignment

You can arrange a group of various sized pictures with the tops aligned along an imaginary horizontal line (figure 20).

Figure 21

Bottoms in Alignment

You can arrange a group of various sized pictures with the bottoms aligned along an imaginary horizontal line (figure 21).

Combination Alignment

You can arrange a group of various sized pictures with the tops and bottoms aligned in two rows (figure 22). Line up the outside edges, as well.

Figure 22

Four Corners

You can make a pleasing arrangement by putting the four largest pictures into the corners of your defined space (figure 23). Then use your smaller pictures to fill in (figure 24).

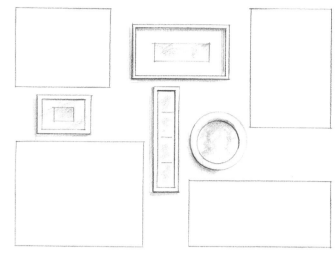

Figure 23

Figure 24

the edge off. (You can soften things up the same way in an off-the-wall display. Add some rounded accessories to soften the harsh angles of a tabletop grouping.) This illustration borrows from the best of both the formal and informal style worlds.

Mosaic

Can you guess why this illustration (figure 25) looks so ordered and well balanced, yet still maintains a sense of informality? The first secret of this mosaic arrangement is that the bottoms of some of the frames are aligned with the tops of others. And notice how a few of the left edges are aligned? A couple of the pictures are actually centered over the others. The other secret? All those right angles can make for a very rigid and serious presentation, but the addition of round, oval, even octagonal-shaped frames really takes

Figure 25

Gallery Style

▼ Here's a great way to hang identically framed pictures all in a neat row, with equal space in between. This method is well suited for contemporary pictures. Apply it to vertical rows (columns), as well. Antiques and older pieces look particularly nice hung vertically.

1. First, define your picture hanging area. Measure and mark the top margin of this area with string and push pins from corner to corner (figure 26.) Measure and mark the center point of the top margin.

2. Hang the two outer pictures. Make sure they are lined up along the top margin. Use a level if needed (figure 27).

3. If you have an odd number of pictures to hang, hang the next one in the middle, centered at the center point of the top margin (figure 28).

4. If you have an even number of pictures to hang, measure the distance remaining between your outer frames.

5. Next, measure the total width of the remaining frames you have left to hang. Subtract this number from the distance remaining between the outer frames.

6. Divide the remainder from step 5 by the number of spaces between frames.

7. Divide the remainder from step 6 by two.

8. Return to the center point you marked in step 1. Measure and mark the amount you got in step 7 to both sides of the center point.

9. Hang the two remaining pictures with their inside edges aligned with the marks you made in step 8 (figure 29). Your pictures are now perfectly spaced.

(Note: If you have more than three or four pictures, repeat the process to fill in, on either side of center.)

Figure 26

Figure 27

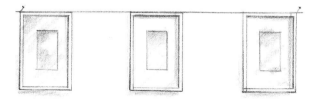

Figure 28

Figure 29

Hanging Hardware

A wide variety of packaged picture hanging hardware is available at craft stores, hardware stores, and at your local frame shop.

Screw eyes are fixed to the back of the frame, and picture wire is strung between them. (See page 42 for details.) *D-rings* act the same as screw eyes, only they lay flat against the back of the frame. To determine where to attach the eyes or rings to your frame, measure the total height of your frame and divide by four. Screw the eyes in this distance from the top of the frame. Heavy frames should be wired with screw eyes about one-third of the way down from the top edge of the frame.

A good alternative to wire is the *sawtooth hanger*. These hangers are well suited to lightweight (less than 8 x 10-inch [20 x 25 cm]) pieces. Make sure you use thin tungsten steel nails with these. They create the smallest holes and do the least damage to walls.

Another alternative to wire is *decorative screw-in fixtures*. These attractive rings are screwed directly into the top of your frame. Be careful with these because it's easy to split the wood if you use a fixture that's too large for your frame. Always drill a starter hole, and make sure you drill into the thickest part of the frame.

While it might be tempting to just use plain old nails, you really should use *picture hangers*. Hangers are inexpensive and available in a variety of sizes appropriate to picture weights. Picture hangers are more supportive than just using nails and are much less likely to fail. The angled nail provides a secure hold in wood, drywall, and plaster. When hanging pictures on a plaster wall, drill a small angled starter hole to make sure you penetrate the wooden lath underneath. If you're hanging an extraordinarily heavy piece, or if you want to hang a piece on a brick or masonry wall, you'll definitely want to use *masonry* screws and *hangers*.

Hanger Position

After you've done your floor exercises and decided on the perfect arrangement, you need to determine exactly where to position the picture hangers on the wall.

1. Mark your wall at the center point of the top of the picture frame you're going to hang.

2. Pull your picture hanging wire taut towards the top of your frame. Measure the distance between the highest point in the wire and the top of your frame.

3. Now, go back to the mark you made on the wall and measure down the distance determined in step 2. Mark this point.

4. Position the picture hanger so the bottom of it is aligned with the mark you just made. Nail in place and hang your picture.

(Note: For a heavy picture that requires two hangers, follow the above procedure, except in step 2 pull your picture wire taut at two points towards the top of your frame. Measure the distance between the horizontal portion of the wire and the top of your frame. Then proceed as instructed above.)

Dragonfly Template

Glossary

Acid-free: Having a pH factor of 7 or higher.

Core: The interior portion of mat board. The core is generally white, or lightly brownish, but it can also be black or a solid color that contrasts the face color.

Bevel: Refers to the 45-degree edge of a mat window. A mat cutter is the tool used to make a bevel cut.

Buffering: Is a process of adding calcium carbonate to wood pulp to neutralize (but not eliminate) the acid. Neutralized board is board that has been buffered.

Burnishing tool: Originally made of bone, this is a smooth tool that is used to "rub out" an overcut mat.

Float mount: Artwork is directly mounted to an attractive mount board. Either no decorative mat is used or at least 1/4 inch (6mm) is left between the artwork and the mat, so that the edges of the artwork are visible. Deckle edged artwork is often mounted in this manner.

Foam core: A type of very lightweight rigid board often used as a mount and/or backing board. The core is made from polystyrene, which is resilient and resists denting. Foam core is available in acid-free and different widths, and with a self-adhesive surface.

French mats: Lines are drawn around the mat window and a light wash is applied in between the lines.

Glazing: Refers to either frame-quality glass or acrylic.

Mat blank: A piece of mat board that has been cut to the correct outside dimension, but hasn't had a window cut into it.

Miter: The joints of a picture frame are miter cut at 45° angles.

Moulding: (also molding) Lengths of decorative wood with special recesses that are cut and joined to make a picture frame.

Mounting Corners and Strips: Pieces of polyester film with acid-free adhesive backing used for mounting artwork. The adhesive never touches the artwork.

Museum Board: 100% cotton rag, acid free, lignin-free board. If museums use it, it's probably good enough for you.

Offset: The bottom border of a mat is wider than the top. Also referred to as "weighing the mat." The bottom width is generally offset by 1/4 to 1/2 inch (6mm to 1.3cm).

Overcut: A term used to describe the corner of a mat window cut beyond the proper stop. A burnishing tool is used to smooth the area and make the cut less conspicuous.

Overlay: The traditional style of matting where the mat board overlaps the artwork by at least 1/8 inch (3mm) on all sides.

Package: The sandwich of glazing, mat, art, mount, and backing to be framed.

Rabbet: The recessed portion of the picture frame into which the package is fit.

Rag: Refers to 100% cotton fiber pulp. This is an acid-free, renewable source.

Reversible: A principle of archival framing. Reversible materials and techniques may not alter the original condition of the artwork.

Spray mounting: A method of permanently mounting artwork with an aerosol spray adhesive.

Thumbnails: Plastic inserts that are used to join the pre-routed moulding.

Undercut: A term used to describe the corner of a mat window cut before the proper stop.